Hanna Stahla

THE MASTER DISCIPLE-MAKER

Hanna S. Shahin, PhD

WestBow
PRESS
A DIVISION OF THOMAS NELSON

WestBow Press books may be ordered through booksellers or by contacting:

WestBow Press
A Division of Thomas Nelson
1663 Liberty Drive
Bloomington, IN 47403
www.westbowpress.com
1-(866) 928-1240

Because of the dynamic nature of the Internet, any web addresses or links contained in this book may have changed since publication and may no longer be valid. The views expressed in this work are solely those of the author and do not necessarily reflect the views of the publisher, and the publisher hereby disclaims any responsibility for them.

Certain stock imagery © Thinkstock.
Any people depicted in stock imagery provided by Thinkstock are models, and such images are being used for illustrative purposes only.

Scripture taken from the Holy Bible, New International Version®. Copyright © 1973, 1978, 1984 Biblica. Used by permission of Zondervan. All rights reserved.

ISBN: 978-1-4497-3130-4 (sc)
ISBN: 978-1-4497-3131-1 (hc)
ISBN: 978-1-4497-3129-8 (e)
Library of Congress Control Number: 2011960353

Printed in the United States of America

WestBow Press rev. date: 11/18/2011

ADVANCE PRAISE FOR
THE MASTER DISCIPLE-MAKER

Hanna Shahin delivers new and fresh truths from the disciple-making process of the greatest, most effective Disciple Maker ever—the Lord Jesus Christ. Prepare to be challenged—from the opening chapter, where Hanna shares fascinating details of his own ministry development, to the final and fresh insights regarding every believer's involvement in the ministry of glorifying Jesus Christ—to the ends of the world!

Stephen Davey. MDiv, STM, DD
Senior Pastor, Colonial Baptist Church
President, Shepherds Theological Seminary
Principal Bible Teacher, Wisdom for the Heart

As a teacher of biblical interpretation, I am very pleased to recommend this book. I believe the Lord has given Dr. Shahin wonderful insights into the interpretation of Jesus' life and ministry and especially His masterful plan of evangelism and discipleship. Not many of us are willing to take on the task of living with a group of new believers day and night as Jesus did. It certainly would disrupt family life! However, the principles are sound. Discipling as Jesus did it requires huge amounts of time spent with the learners. Daws Trotman learned that secret years ago and passed it on to the Navigators. Dr. Robert Coleman, in his book, *The Master Plan of Evangelism,* also emphasized that point. I especially like the concept of "the greater commission" of so living as to bring greater glory to God. This is the ultimate goal for each of our lives.

Dr. David W. King, ThD, LLD

Making disciples is the heart of the Great Commission. Yet today, so few Christians really know what it means to make a disciple, much less have any fruit to show for it. How sad is this? What are people going to say when they get to heaven and have never made a single disciple? God bless Hanna Shahin, therefore, for writing this book! His love for God's Word and for teaching people how to obey it shines through on every page. There is no formula for making disciples, but the principles Hanna lays out from the Scriptures and his own practical experience—especially in North Africa and the Middle East—will help anyone seeking to obey the Great Commission in this generation.

Joel C. Rosenberg, *New York Times* best-selling author of *Epicenter* and *Inside the Revolution*

Have you ever thought why our methods of discipling new believers do not work as well as we have hoped? Have you ever thought why these new believers were not more up to Bible reading, study, and prayer? Have you ever asked yourself why the first generation of believers in Jesus in New Testament times have turned the world of the Mediterranean Basin upside down? If you have asked yourself such kind of questions, then this book is for you!

Dr. Hanna Shahin, from personal experience with the "Soccer Church" in F'heis (Jordan), shows how Jesus meant it to be: the interaction between disciple and discipler, trainee and trainer, or mentoree and mentor. What he shows is the difference between propositional discipling and incarnational discipling. The cost for the trainer is high, but the results are worth the efforts. This book is bound to leave a changing impact on many who are active in the missions field, allowing them to come back to more biblical approaches of discipler for making disciples, "the Jesus style": this process involves a radical lifestyle change for the discipler.

Jurg Loeliger, MS, PhD
Corseaux, Switzerland

Hanna Shahin opens new vistas in our consideration of Jesus ministry and objectives. While God has used evangelistic methods to reach unbelievers, the preparation of young believers one to one or in small group settings seems to be an effective method of teaching. By His words and life, Jesus taught the Word and the passion of His mission here on earth. Indeed, He was a master disciple maker!

Tom Lowell, D Litt
Chairman, Trans World Radio Board of Directors

Every now and then I appreciate reading a book by someone "who gets it." Hanna Shahin has captured the essence of the impartation of one's spiritual pilgrimage to another person. He demonstrates that being a disciple is many times "caught" and not "taught."

I've spent over 30 years asking God to develop disciples and leaders. *The Master Disciple-Maker* resonates with the reality of personally seeing this happen.

Lauren Libby
International President, TWR International

As a committed discipler of men for the Kingdom of our Lord and having known Hanna Shahin and his family for over three decades, I thoroughly enjoyed reading *The Master Disciple-Maker* and gained new insights on the teaching of Jesus on what He Himself was committed to during His lifetime on earth. Hanna, who was born and grew up and played and walked in the very same towns and cities as our Lord Jesus did, and with his lifelong experience in discipling men and women for Jesus, will give you a fresh look on the very stories and parables Jesus used in discipling the first apostles of the church. You will get the feeling you are reading them for the first time ever.

Henri Aoun
Director, LifeAgape International

"Take delight in the Lord, and He will give you the desires of your heart" (Psalm 37:4). How does that happen and what does that really mean? Reading this book to me was a clear illustration of what we as followers of Christ should do: study, meditate, take time, and let the

Word of God water our souls. We hunger for spiritual fulfillment but often don't do anything to obtain it. We seek in all the wrong places, and that is why we don't find it. This book is a great study in what Jesus and the disciples had to do and why. It is a call to all of us back to the founding principles of our faith.

Salem Shahin, MD

DEDICATION

To my friend and former pastor, the Reverend Fawaz Ameish of Amman, Jordan, and his wife, Ruthie, who opened their hearts and home to our family, and who modeled in their lives the love and life of Christ before us.

PREFACE

The book you are holding in your hands was much easier for me to write than for you its reader or for me to apply. This is the case, because words, voided of their day-to-day application, are, after all, simply words, letters combined together to make sense. But unless they translate into life, the residual effect of writing or reading them can be very minimal.

We will learn in this book—without going into every little detail—what it meant for the Lord to make disciples out of the twelve men He called to follow Him. For while they were called disciples early on, yet it took more than three years of teaching, of prodding, and most important, of living the message of the Kingdom before their very eyes before they could be entrusted to carry that message to the world. And even then, were it not for the outpouring of the Holy Spirit on the day of Pentecost, they probably would have bickered among themselves, as they did while their Lord was still with them, that they would have failed in their mission even before starting.

This book outlines the method that Jesus uniquely used, which was to teach by example rather than propositionally. He lived out His teachings with and before His followers in the same way that we, as fathers and mothers, also live out our lives before our own children. We prayed with them and played with them before teaching them how to pray or play. We walked and talked before them and with them before actually teaching them how to do either. Yet, somewhere in the course of life, we forget these basic principles and rather than follow the same pattern of living out the message—of becoming the message—we begin to carry it on our tongues or present it in books, and thus, the message loses its power.

As you make your way to the last chapter or two, a shocking surprise awaits you. In those last pages, I unpack the Great Commission for us, confront us with what Jesus was really commissioning His disciples to do, and then connect that with what I call the *Greater Commission* that the Father commissioned the Son to do, which, according to John 17:4, was making disciples.

As you conclude reading this book, you will begin to wonder whether the Twelve really understood their mission, and as important, you will begin to ask yourself whether you and I have understood our true mission in life thus far. My prayer is that through the reading of this book, you will gain a better understanding of what that mission is and that you will have the same passion to go out and make it happen. I hope you will reach the same conclusion I have reached as you read this book, which is the fact that evangelism alone will not win the world to Christ. Making disciples does.

Hanna S. Shahin, PhD
President and Founder
Endure International, Inc

INTRODUCTION

DISCIPLESHIP OR DISCIPLE-MAKING

Definitions of the term "discipleship" are not lacking in Christian circles. Generally speaking, discipleship is understood to mean helping younger Christians mature in Christ, whether by gaining a better understanding of the Word of God or by becoming more committed to the cause of Christ and His church, thus being better equipped to serve Him. Another way of stating this would be that discipleship purposes to assist younger Christians to become more like Christ.

The notion of discipleship has gained traction and emphasis in the last couple of decades, which has led a number of Evangelical para-church organizations, as well as denominations, to design and/or compile materials they identify as discipleship courses. These are usually steps or lessons that a mentor, a discipler, or a mature Christian guides a newer or younger Christian to complete. They cover topics such as learning how to hear God speak, discovering the principles of spiritual growth, how to have a happy marriage, and other important aspects in the life of a Christian.

The term "disciple-making" is used less in Christian circles than the term "discipleship." And when used, it mostly refers—though not always—to similar processes and procedures as in discipleship, thus making both terms almost interchangeable. The question is whether this is a proper biblical understanding of what disciple-making really involves.

One big difference this book seeks to demonstrate is that, contrary to the general perception and practice, biblical disciple-making is a process that is initiated with nonbelievers first. Only secondarily does the discipleship process develop into assisting younger believers to mature in Christ. Another big difference that this book will advance is that biblical disciple-making is incarnational rather than propositional. This important aspect will become very clear, as we study the model that Jesus set before us in the four Gospels.

This book looks exclusively at the disciple-making process that the Lord Jesus Christ used with His Twelve. It does not go into the book of Acts to see whether Peter, Paul, or the other disciples applied the same methodology or part thereof in their ministry. Needless to say, the book of Acts is not disciple-making material. This is not the emphasis that Luke sought to present. However, this does not take away from whatever disciple-making principles a Bible student may glean from that book.

It also needs to be said that this book does not look into ways and means of getting better results from the disciple-making process, nor does the book guarantee the model that was used by the Lord according to the Gospels will bring about the type of disciples hoped for. The next paragraph will touch on that.

While this book is not about promoting the Person or the Power of the Holy Spirit of God, it ought to be stated and restated up front that outside an infilling of the Third Person of the Trinity, no amount of discipleship or disciple-making, regardless of the means used— whether incarnational or propositional—would ever bring forth the desired fruit. This would also be true regardless of the materials used as well as regardless of the discipler using it. The Lord Jesus Himself confirmed that outside the power of the promised Holy Spirit, His own work with the disciples would have come to naught. As an example, it suffices to observe the disciples even after the Lord is raised from the dead and before the day of Pentecost. Many, beginning with Peter, went back to their old fishing practice. Not much had changed, even after three plus years of constant prodding.

On the other hand, the Lord promised that with the advent of the Holy Spirit, His disciples would be able to do greater things than He Himself did. In the final analysis, the secret is not in the methodology, but it is in a life controlled by the Spirit of God.

CHAPTER I

THE SOCCER CHURCH

The year was 1976. My family and I had recently moved from Lebanon to Egypt to Jordan. We came as refugees. The Lebanese civil war had forced hundreds of thousands out of their homes and jobs. My family and I were part of those casualties. As it was, none were spared, especially foreign workers like ourselves. Outside of a secure job at the Baptist Center for Radio and Television in a small town overlooking the capital city, Beirut, nothing else was secure. My daily commute was laden with risk. If it was not shelling, it was sniper fire. Having been born into a Palestinian Christian background, I was a potential enemy to both sides of the Lebanese strife, now turned into a full-fledged civil war. To the Palestinian and Lebanese Muslim fighters, I was Christian, and to the Lebanese Christian phalangists, I was Palestinian. My young wife and child were not much safer at home, which led me at times to drive them to a safer haven: a friend's home in Baalbek, spared from the atrocities of Beirut. Our young son's nightly nightmares, combined with our daytime nightmares, finally drove us out. Initially, we found refuge in Egypt, and in the spring of 1976, we moved to Jordan. And since we carried Jordanian passports, we became like refugees in our own country!

On arriving in Jordan in March of that year, my first thought was to look for a church I could pastor. Church pastoring was not my first love. A few years before, while still finishing my seminary training in Lebanon, a church in Jordan had invited me to take up that role.

But back then, I declined. My thought was, *Why would I want to go take over another's church? Why would I want to inherit the former pastor's problems and challenges?* Plus, I was not a gifted preacher. I had a very hard time preaching once a month or less. Preaching weekly would make my life miserable, if not intolerable. That was my thinking then.

But now, things had drastically changed. The months my family and I stayed in Egypt after evacuating Lebanon were ones of practical training. The Lord had opened my heart to the Scriptures and had opened the Scriptures to my mind. That enabled me to preach daily for thirteen weeks in a row. Now in Amman as a refugee, unemployed, and running out of cash, I started looking for an empty Baptist church pulpit. But that was not to be. Every empty Baptist and non-Baptist church pulpit had been filled by Lebanese pastors who, like us, had found refuge in Jordan—except they had arrived months before we did. They, unlike us, did not make a several months' detour via Egypt.

Ten days went by, and still there was nothing on the horizon. The small savings we had were being gradually depleted. We were staying at a small motel—if it could be called that—all four of us, our two young sons, my wife and I huddled in one room, eating out every meal, including breakfast. April was around the corner, and the weather was mild, allowing us many hours outside our miserable surroundings at that motel. It was during these frequent outings that, every once in a while, we would accidentally run into other war casualties from Lebanon. We were comforted in our shared pain. We could also vent some of our personal frustrations to these friends and acquaintances. They were living in similar circumstances. As it was, though, we were better off. At least we carried Jordanian passports and did not have to apply for residence permits or visas. But these Lebanese friends and acquaintances could do nothing for themselves or for us in terms of employment. Or so we thought!

Connections in the Arab Middle East, and especially in a country like Jordan, are key to anything and everything. Knowing the right people in the right places can work wonders. As it was, all my Jordanian connections boiled down to just one person, who was not even in the right place. The only person I knew in this country was the pastor of a church. Judging by every outward appearance, my chances of finding a job anytime soon were nonexistent.

Yet, something was being prepared behind the scenes of which I was completely unaware. One of our Lebanese friends, who I had accidentally bumped into in Amman and who was also a war casualty, was visiting Mr. Hanna Hashweh, the manager of the British Airways sales agent office. During their visit, my name came up, and before we knew it, Mr. Hashweh was at our door, offering me a position at their sales office.

The idea of looking for an empty pulpit vanished as quickly as it had crossed my mind, and before I knew it, something else popped up. Another acquaintance from our years in Lebanon, Mr. Antoine Dib, came to our small, one-room apartment one day and asked us to consider moving out of the capital city, Amman, to a neighboring town called F'heis. Having only been a few months in Jordan, I had no clue where, how big, or how modern that town was.

Moving from a modern, two-bedroom apartment in bustling Beirut to an old, beaten, one-room facility in a quieter Amman neighborhood was enough adjustment for the time being, one might think. And the invitation to move to a small town on the outskirts of Amman was not going to make things any easier. We had never lived in Jordan before, let alone in a rural area. We were not familiar with the customs and traditions of small-town people. Yet, there was a real reason to go, including the reason for the invitation to move: the totally unexpected opportunity to plant a church!

My university education in psychology and philosophy, as well as my seminary training, may have helped me to some degree in becoming a Christian radio speaker, though I came up very short when I first started. That same education might also have helped me pastor a church, especially now that I had the confidence I could preach to an audience. Yet, there was nothing to guide me in how I was to go about planting a church. Our education at the seminary did not have a course on church-planting. Moreover, I had never seen anyone do it. Every church I joined when I was single, and every church we attended or joined as a married couple, had already been planted and well established before we got there. So, I didn't know how to start one. Where should I begin?

In more ways than one, this invitation to plant a church was reminiscent of the invitation given me to become involved in Christian radio, except this one was worse: more sudden, unexpected, and less safe! The audience I would be serving did not live hundreds or thousands of kilometers away. Back then when I was broadcasting, I was sitting in a small radio studio overlooking Beirut, Lebanon, and talking to audiences as far away as Algeria and Morocco, on the distant western shores of the Mediterranean Sea. By moving into a small town to plant a church, my audience would be right before my eyes, and we would be right in front of their eyes to either encourage and emulate or criticize and avoid. In a small town the size of F'heis, my life and that of my young family could become the talk of the townspeople. This is not to say my radio audiences never criticized me, but if they did, it was from afar or behind my back and not in my own backyard.

In my radio years, I could always hide behind the microphone. The audiences liked or disliked my voice. They liked or disliked what I had to say. Yet, they were blind to the way I treated my wife and family. They probably could not care less. They were blind to my appearance: how I looked, what I wore, whether I was clean-shaven or grew a beard, or whether I was hospitable. All these details—and scores more—were nonissues. All that mattered was whether I could provide them company, meaningful company, or even just entertain them.

Not anymore. If I should accept the invitation to go to F'heis to plant a church, I should expect to see my privacy as an individual and our privacy as a family invaded at any time. The notion of privacy does not exist in rural areas in Jordan, nor possibly in any rural area anywhere in the world. Now, why should I be setting myself up for all that?

In my radio years, it was extremely important to be as personable as my voice would allow. It was extremely important to be respectful every time a listener invited me into his home or his car. I knew he had the controls between his fingers. He could shut me off with a simple turn of his radio knob. I was his guest, and I was well aware of that. At least I did my best to be aware of it.

Moving into this small town would completely change the dynamics of every interaction I would have. For a while, I, too, would be a guest, and I would probably be one for years to come—not just for an hour or two a day, as was the case during my radio years. I would be a guest all day every day, year in and year out, or until we decided to call it quits and move out. The audience would not be able to shut me off with the same ease as a radio listener could. Moreover, my new congregation would have a lot more to judge me by than just my words, my tone of voice, or my respect. A smile, a frown, and everything in between could come between my audience and me and build a bridge of trust. Or, they could come between us and put up a wall of distrust. My entire life, not just my words, would be laid out before them to look at and judge.

In radio, I had turned the world and all its imagery into words. The letters of the alphabet became my only paint. And my brush was my skill in mixing this paint and drawing colorful images. I was judged by how skillful I was in breathing life in all its dimensions back into my words. How I influenced the listeners' ears to become not just their means of hearing but also their means of smelling, seeing, and touching, depended to a large extent on my skill as a communicator. This is what we called creating "presence" on the radio.

Planting a new church would involve much more than "presence." Planting a church in a small town requires much more than communication skills. It requires much more than even knowing one's Bible and knowing it well. It puts one's very life in the balance. One's life becomes the paint and the brush, so to speak. And that will either turn out to be one's greatest asset or one's riskiest liability. Planting a church in a small town is at the core of the notion of incarnation, where the Word of God takes on flesh and blood. Except this is not about fleshing the Word in the life of Jesus! It is fleshing the Word by the example of one's own life.

I asked our friend to give us time to think and pray. Moving to F'heis presented at least one advantage. We could end up with better living conditions, more space—forget modernity—than my limited income could afford us in Amman. My pay at the General Sales Agent office was barely enough to pay for a two—or three-bedroom apartment in Amman. We could rent similar facilities in this small town for less than half the price.

It was not long before we saw our family of four move to F'heis. The neighborhood—if it could be called that—was pretty shabby. There did not seem to be much in terms of planning, at least not in that part of town. Four brothers and a sister had divided their family's lot among them, with each painting his house the way he chose. One house was painted light brown, while another was pinkish, and the third was painted light sky blue. Maybe it was to differentiate them one from the other from a distance.

There was not much in common among the three houses except the absence of architectural engineering. By the looks of it, at least one of the brothers did not seem to have consulted an architect to help him in much of anything. That one house had two main doors to it, and there was no sense in trying to understand why. Yet, and contrary to any logic, that specific design proved to work to our benefit. This is where my wife, two kids, and I ended up. This would become our home for the next couple of years.

Rather than rent us his house—which was a little over one thousand square feet—in its totality, the owner decided to give up everything except the living room, which he and his family continued to occupy. We could rent everything else, which boiled down to a smaller living room on the other end of the house, two bedrooms, one bathroom, and a kitchenette. But at least we had our own main door. At times though, it felt like we shared everything, including our main door. The owner could choose, uninvited, to come through that door and check things out for himself. After all, this was his house; we were only renters. We could choose to lock our front door, but that would be interpreted as being unfriendly and unwelcoming. That also was part of living in rural Jordan!

Connecting the two sections of this one-floor house on the inside was a wooden door. The owner's large living room sat on one side of that door, and our small kitchen immediately behind it. Our neighbors could not only smell the foods that Evelyn cooked, they could also hear who was doing the dishes. Little did we realize how offended the wife would be when she discovered one day that I was washing the dishes. She did not spare her voice, as she came to our door, thumping and rebuking Evelyn for doing that to me.

The same scenario would be repeated, though to a lesser degree, over other issues. I could not hold our baby and feed him, and obviously, I was not supposed to change his diapers. And if I was holding him and he cried, Evelyn was expected to take him from me immediately, or the neighbor's wife would come and literally grab him from my hands and care for him. To our neighbors, man's world and woman's world were very well defined, and no crossover was permissible.

Within a few hours of our arrival, we discovered that we were not really living with just one family, or even sharing our part of the house with them; rather, we were living within a closely knit family neighborhood. There were no walls, no fences, and no trees, not just between these three houses, but also between them and the next set of houses all around them. This is where other members of their extended family lived. This was really a clan, and we found ourselves in the midst of it. Something as simple as knowing people's names became quite complex. There were quite a few and the list went on and on. And, of course, one could not greet one person without greeting the others. Befriending one automatically meant befriending everyone else, and if we lost the trust of one, God help us!

The absence of walls or fences within the context of this clan translated into other relational dimensions, with potential benefits and risks involved. Any action or reaction on our part, whether factual or perceived, would be interpreted and reinterpreted in every house and on every tongue. There were no barriers of any sort. We did not have the liberty to live behind closed doors, not in rural Jordan, for the small community would have plenty to say!

Language experts tell us that immersion is the best means of learning a new language, or in this case, a dialect. Jordan—then a country of less than five million inhabitants—like other Arab Middle Eastern countries, spoke Arabic. But that identification can be misleading. Egypt also speaks Arabic, as well as Lebanon, Sudan, and Morocco, among many other nations. But in each case, the Arabic is quite different. Moroccan Arabic, for one, called Darija, is hardly understood by most other Arabic speakers except Algerians. The Egyptian dialect is probably the most widely understood, thanks to its widespread works of art in song, theater, and cinema.

Coming from and having been immersed in the Lebanese dialect for seven consecutive years, our accent sounded foreign to Jordanians. In the same way, the Jordanian dialect sounded new to us, especially in the countryside. As it was, and as we expected, there was quite a bit of adjustment to living in rural Jordan, whether in terms of dialect or culture in general.

We settled in and began our lives in F'heis. Dressed in my ironed white shirt, dark blue uniform, tie, and hat, I began making the daily return trip to Amman. Service taxis—where four or five passengers each pays a fixed fare—made the trip in less than twenty minutes. Once in downtown Amman, I would ride another service taxi to the Intercontinental Hotel, which is where the British Airways GSA offices were located. I worked from eight in the morning until four or five in the afternoon, after which I made my way back home, again using the same means of transportation.

By the time I walked from where the taxi dropped me off in town until I reached our home—a good half-mile dirt road—I had usually shook half a dozen hands and waved at another half-dozen people. I did not stand out: my dark uniform and hat did. And possibly my foreign, Lebanese accent.

While still in the distance, I could hear the kids of the neighborhood shouting after each other, and there were quite a few. The majority of them were in their early teens. They would be out in the field, running, kicking a ball, or simply trying to have a good time. Their moms and dads did not mind seeing their kids playing in the dirt; they probably wanted some quiet at home. Every once in a while, a fight would erupt, and the moms and dads would be dragged into it as well.

I was never much into sports. In my school days in Jerusalem, I was into playing snooker and table tennis at the school or at local clubs. And though I liked volleyball, given my small size, my chances of getting a spot in the game at school were always slim. I learned to enjoy watching the game. I still do.

Watching the neighborhood kids playing in the open field brought back memories of my childhood at the Catholic orphanage in Bethany, east of Jerusalem. There was not much grass there, either. There, too, we would be outside, playing in the dirt, kicking the ball, or just passing time. And it was usually the latter. The sisters at the orphanage could not afford enough balls to keep the thirty or so boys happy and occupied.

My age would have been about the same as these boys': maybe a little younger than many of them. Like these boys here, we also got into fights, though probably not as often. Boys will always be boys, regardless of age, especially when left on their own, as those neighborhood kids were. Moms were not going to play ball with their boys. Nor would dads. Playing ball or running around barefoot in an open field is not what dads are made of or for, not in rural Jordan. A dad could lose his self-respect and the respect of his neighbors if he were to do such a thing. Dads don't wear shorts and T-shirts. They don't wear tennis shoes. They probably did not have tennis shoes, shorts, or T-shirts, not because they could not afford them, but because they just had no use for them at their age.

I reviewed my situation. After all, I was a stranger. My accent betrayed me every time I opened my mouth. I knew I did not quite belong, and everyone else in the neighborhood knew that much. What shame or disrespect would I bring on my family and myself if I were to get involved in the lives of these young boys? I had shorts, and I had T-shirts. All I would need was a pair of tennis shoes, and I could be out playing with those kids.

There I was. I was an adult, married, and father of two young boys. My neighbors and those around them did not even call me by my first name, Hanna. They called me "Abu Bassem," or, "father of Bassem" (Bassem being our firstborn son). Addressing a married man by the word "Abu" is always a sign of respect. But also of age. I was not a child anymore.

Additionally, I worked in a very respectable job. Even my dark blue uniform demanded respect. Moreover, I came here with a purpose. I came to plant a church. What business did I have taking off my outward sign of respect, my blue uniform, and putting on a T-shirt, a pair of shorts, and tennis shoes? Even if I were not going to go out and play with the kids, I would still be looked down at. How would I even venture to visit with my neighbors? This is so contrary to culture and to tradition. What chance would I have to influence them?

The adults that we lived among were probably already set in their ways. They had their religious, denominational, and cultural traditions. My dark blue uniform could help earn me some respect and a listening ear once in a while, but it was doubtful that it could go far enough to bridge these many gaps.

So there I was, torn between two seemingly good goals: standing tall as a man and seeking to influence the men in our neighborhood, or taking off the garb, becoming a kid, and getting involved in the lives of kids. The ultimate goal did not change. It was still to see a church planted in that town. I was only seeking guidance as to where I should start. In many ways, I knew where my heart was, but I did not have the courage to follow it. I needed something to tip it.

One day, as usual, the service taxi dropped me at the edge of the dirt road. As usual, I stopped to shake a few hands and wave at others. As usual, the neighborhood boys were out playing. That must have become a sacred, daily tradition. My family and I had been there a couple of months, and if anything, the number of boys playing soccer was increasing almost by the day. Yet, there was a noticeable difference that day in June. From a distance, I could see a female figure carrying a baby. The closer I got, the more pronounced was the face.

It was Evelyn, my wife, holding our youngest son, Shadi, then only a few months old.

What I could not see from a distance was a new player; the reason that forced Evelyn out of the house. Out in the field, trying his luck to kick the ball, was Bassem. He was three and quite small for his age. Evelyn could not trust him to the older kids. She had to go out and watch over him.

All of a sudden, it dawned on me: our son Bassem gave me the excuse, or maybe the reason! With a young child in her arms, Evelyn could not be expected to be out in the field, roughing it with the neighborhood kids. There was a need for a male figure, willing to give time, attention, and exercise control. Plus, I now had a son who wanted to be out with the big boys. He also wanted to share in the fun.

Without giving in to other considerations, I went into the house, took off my blue uniform, put on a pair of shorts, T-shirt, and tennis shoes and within minutes was out again. My son had unknowingly helped tip the balance.

The boys of the neighborhood were as ecstatic as they were shocked. They had their dads and uncles with them all these years, but not one dared to do what this "stranger" did. Yet, in their eyes also, here was a man validating their youthful quest for sports and fun by wanting to join in.

Up 'til those moments, there had not been much communication between me and these boys, except maybe when on a rare occasion a ball would land close to me, as I walked through their playing field on my way home from work. I remember hitting a ball or two. But nothing much beyond that.

Now, I was in their midst. I did not quite belong, but they realized that I was trying. It probably required as much adjustment for them to see a man playing ball with them as it required of me. And while it was true that I was validating their youthful quest for fun, I was also intruding into their world. In their turn, they also had to accept me.

11

Accepting my age was one thing. Accepting and adapting to my speed, or to the lack of it, was another. Accepting my intrusion was one thing. Accepting my skill, or its absence, was another. I could not possibly keep pace with them. I probably fell a time or two, as I tried to control a passing ball. To me, that was no laughing matter. But to them it was, except that they were more controlled and forgiving.

By taking off my long pants, my dress shoes, and my uniform shirt, and putting on shorts and tennis shoes and going out to their playground, I had allowed myself to be seen and perceived as a kid. I either had to accept being treated like one, or go back inside and put on my normal garb.

One of the first challenges we faced was how they would address me. I knew their individual names, and they knew mine. They had heard their families talk about Abu Bassem and Om Bassem (father and mother of Bassem). But those terms were too formal. They were not quite fitting for the playground. I could sense their hesitation, and I felt I had to let them feel at ease. So, as soon as the first occasion presented itself, I asked them to call me the same thing their parents did.

For about an hour, we played a very humble version of soccer. I didn't score any goals. For one thing, the goals kept shifting. But that was beside the point. The objective was to break the ice, begin to build a sense of camaraderie, and start some type of involvement in the lives of these boys. All that and more was being started that afternoon and evening. A sense of victory swept over me. I succeeded in overcoming my own fears, doubts, and trepidation. First steps are always the hardest. I was glad I took that first step.

Dark was setting in, and I was ready for a break. And since the kids had already been playing long before I got there, they were ready to call it a day. In the meantime, Evelyn was home, preparing something to eat. No sooner had she realized that we were done playing than she invited the whole bunch into our home. She served us all hot chocolate and homemade, freshly baked biscuits. And for the next thirty minutes or so, we all relived the feats and marvelous moments of the game, with each player trying to outdo the other. It sounded like we were playing for the World Cup.

It was time to wrap up. I asked if we could take just a moment and lift a prayer of thanks to God that no one was seriously hurt and for the good time we had. With my eyes and their eyes open, I said a brief prayer. As they all stood to go, one of the group turned around and asked, "Will you play again with us tomorrow?"

Without even pausing to think, I replied, "I will, if you let me." With a big smile on his face, he turned away and left.

Day in and day out, week after week, and month after month, we practiced and played. Day in and day out, we crowded into our small living room, drank hot chocolate, ate cookies, chatted, prayed, and, over time, started reading the Bible together. Those young boys were growing, both physically and in their understanding of the Word. Pretty soon, our living room was too small to hold their number.

All of a sudden, I had a name change. Not the kids, but the parents started calling me "Gassees," pastor in Jordanian Arabic. I was still dressing up in my dark blue uniform and working in the airline industry. I did not have a church. And though the boys were gradually growing out of their soccer tradition, I was still playing with them when they did. So, where in the world did I get that name?

Walking home from work one day, one of the dads stopped me. His house was halfway between the main road and our small lodging. He and his family belonged to the same clan. His two sons were regularly part of our soccer teams. They were also part of our small, home, Bible study group. Weeks before, they had taken the initiative and invited us to go meet their parents, which we did. But that was the end of it. Or so we thought. I was about to pass the dad's house that day, when all of a sudden, I heard him call from below, "Gassees. Gassees." His house was a few feet below street level.

I stopped and turned to meet him. He came over, shook my hand, and said, "I hear that you do not have much room for the group that meets in your home. I am offering my house to you. It is yours to use as often and as long as you need." I was overwhelmed. I had not imagined the impact that our life would have on these kids, let alone on their parents. Taking the neighbor up on his offer, we started having weekly Bible study meetings in his home.

But our house continued to be open for everything else, as were our hearts. Our relationship with these kids and with their parents grew by the day. At six or a little before six in the morning, our nostrils would be filled with the smell of a wood fire. Soon after, and on a daily basis, our next-door neighbor's wife would knock on our door and hand Evelyn a couple of freshly made loaves of bread. She knew I left early to go to work, and she wanted to make sure I had the first loaf of bread. We were no longer neighbors. We had become one large family.

Three fruitful years passed. It was not too long after that when our number outgrew the large living room that the neighbor had offered. By then, not only did our soccer teams attend our regular meetings of Bible study, their sisters and other family members joined in as well. We moved out to rented facilities in town.

I did not realize the full impact of becoming a kid like those kids; of going out every day and playing ball with them; of chatting, eating, praying, and studying God's Word with them. I did my part, and Evelyn did her part in seeding these young hearts with the Word of God and with Christian values, but God was giving the growth. It was out of this neighborhood that a "soccer" church was planted in the rural town of F'heis in Jordan. Those same young men, in effect, would grow to be the firstfruits of the F'heis Baptist Church.

Following those three years, from 1976 to 1979, an interruption occurred, and our family moved to Africa for the next few months. On our return to Jordan, we saw ourselves settle in Amman again rather than in the town of F'heis. Our oldest son, Bassem, was six and ready to go to school.

Did we make a mistake in settling in Amman? Should we have gone back to that small town to continue doing what we did before? I don't know that *we* can settle these questions in our minds. For even though we began making regular visits to the town, and while a ministry to younger children was also added with members from the Amman Baptist Church becoming involved, our out-of-town ministering to the church was never as successful or rewarding as it had been when we lived in F'heis. Meanwhile, I assumed managerial responsibilities for a para-church organization and served as associate pastor of the main Baptist church in Amman.

In 1983, our family was on the move again, this time to Europe, where we would be involved one more time and for the next twenty-three years in Christian radio. (More on that in my book, *My Enemy . . . My Brother.*) Our life and ministry in Jordan generally, and most specifically in F'heis, would be relegated to memory. The memory of those boys running around and the smell of that fresh bread will continue to bless us. In many ways, we wish we could live them over again and again!

Yet, for all those sweet memories and despite my frequent travels from Europe to the Middle East, and to Jordan in particular, I often failed to take time to go back and visit with that soccer church. There were very long, inexcusable intervals between my sporadic visits. It was not until the summer of 2006 that I finally decided to honor the church's invitation and spend a week preaching at that church.

Many of the faces were new to me. I was again trying to learn new names, while others' I was trying to remember. There was quite a group of mostly younger married men, some with their wives, and some without. There were also a good number of women with younger children.

I took a seat in one of the pews, bent my head, and did my best to hide my emotions while wiping away a tear or two. Not in my wildest imagination would I have thought that the seeds we planted thirty years ago could bear such fruit. This was not the work of man.

A lieutenant colonel sat behind the piano. Another gentleman stood to lead in song. This would be the first of a weeklong series of evangelistic meetings, mostly meant to invite the audience to turn back to God. The song leader started by welcoming members and visitors. Then, out of the blue, came his announcement: "With us here today, we have a very special guest: our soccer captain and coach, Reverend Hanna 'Maradona.'"

Hussam, the song leader, was one of the first boys, probably aged nine or ten at the time, to have joined our soccer team. He had grown to be a man and a leader in the church. Hussam was running his own business. Mohsen, the lieutenant colonel playing the piano, was his brother. Jiries, Ra'ed, Khaled, and a half dozen other men now leading the church—some of them established businessmen, others doing other things—were also part of that first team of players! I could not hold back my tears anymore. I was not prepared for this. I could not find enough words of gratitude to the Lord for what He had done and continued to do. Those three years or more of disciple-making were not spent in vain. They were worth abandoning the big city for this small, rural town with it customs and traditions. They were worth the embarrassment of putting on shorts, of running like a kid, of falling down trying to catch a ball, and every other aspect of getting involved in the lives of these once young boys, now turned mature and adult men. It was well worth it all and more.

CHAPTER II

New Testament Disciples

In the New Testament, the word "disciple" appears a little fewer that three hundred times. The vast majority of references to the term "disciple" is made in connection with the twelve followers of the Lord Jesus. Of the remaining number, there are a few references to followers of other leaders, such as John the Baptist, who had his own disciples, or to the Pharisees, who also had their disciples. In one instance, we read of the Pharisees referring to themselves as disciples of Moses (see John 9:28). The other uses of the term refer to followers of the Lord other than the Twelve. The Gospels and the book of Acts introduce us to those others without necessarily giving us too many details about them. Let us examine some of these citations where the term "disciple" is used but does not refer to the Twelve.

One of those other disciples is Joseph of Arimathea, in whose tomb the body of Jesus was buried. Mark and Luke, in their gospels, describe Joseph as someone, "waiting for the kingdom of God" (see Mark 15:43, and Luke 23:50-52). Matthew and John, on the other hand, expressly speak of him as a disciple of Jesus (see Matthew 27:57 and John 19:38).

In the Gospel according to Luke (Luke 6:17), we read the following: "He, [that is, Jesus] went down with them and stood on a level place. A large crowd of his disciples was there and a great number of people from all over Judea, from Jerusalem, and from the coast of Tyre and Sidon."

In Luke 19:37, we read: "When he came near the place where the road goes down the Mount of Olives, the whole crowd of disciples began joyfully to praise God in loud voices for all the miracles they had seen."

The twelve were by no means a large crowd. One can hardly describe them as a crowd, let alone a large crowd. It would be awkward for Luke to make such a claim in the verses above if he were only referring to the twelve. Such terminology leaves little room except to believe that Jesus had a much larger number of disciples than the familiar twelve.

John corroborates that notion in his gospel. In John 6:66, we read, "From this time many of his disciples turned back and no longer followed him."

We know that this verse does not refer in any way to the twelve. So, who were those other disciples who turned their backs on Jesus and ceased following Him, and what was their number, wherein John speaks of them as many?

Chapter 6 of the book of Acts begins: "In those days when the number of disciples was increasing, the Grecian Jews among them complained against the Hebraic Jews because their widows were being overlooked in the daily distribution of food. So the Twelve gathered all the disciples together and said it would not be right for us to neglect the ministry of the word of God in order to wait on tables" (Acts 6:1-2).

In verse 7 of the same chapter, we read, "So the word of God spread. The number of disciples in Jerusalem increased rapidly, and a large number of priests became obedient to the faith" (Acts 6:7).

In Acts 9:10, Luke calls Ananias a disciple. A few verses later, he refers to the "disciples in Damascus" (Acts 9:19). Then, in Acts 9:36, he calls Tabitha a disciple, and two verses after that, he talks of the disciples in Joppa (Acts 9:38).

In short, the multiple citations of the word "disciple" in the book of Acts refer to others besides the twelve.

It is worth noting that the Greek word for all the above does not change, even with the obvious changes in the context of its use. It is the same root word *mathetes* that is every time translated into the English word "disciple," whether it refers to the disciples of John the Baptist, the disciples of the Pharisees, or the disciples of Jesus. And the English meaning of that word is simply "learner."

One could argue that, historically, references to disciples—whether based on the New Testament, previous Greek literature, or writings contemporary to the times of our Lord—imply the idea of adhering to the teachings of a great master, though this may not necessarily be stated. Yet, that idea is not inherently true of that term. Such an idea was governed by the type of relationship that existed between a certain teacher or master and his follower or disciple. In other words, it could simply have denoted a learner or a pupil, and it could have denoted a committed adherent or a state somewhere between the two.

The notion of master/disciple was not new in the days of our Lord. Religious as well as political and philosophical leaders had followers of their own, who, like the followers of Jesus, were also designated by the term "disciple" or similar names.

Based on the above, we can safely assume that the word "disciple" in the Gospels in its reference to the disciples of Jesus does not automatically mean that the one designated a disciple had, in fact, become either a committed follower or a believer. Otherwise, what would we do with John 6:66, where we read, "From this time many of his disciples turned back and no longer followed him"? Did those disciples believe in Jesus one day and the next, decided to turn back and no longer follow Him? And what do we do with Judas Iscariot, who also was one of the twelve and called disciple?

Is it not more correct to assume that, as in the case of those who followed John or those who followed the teachings of the Pharisees, the disciples of Jesus similarly followed his teachings without necessarily comprehending or believing who He really was? Would that not better explain their progressive understanding of His true identity and their progressive devotion to Him? Would it not be an overstatement to say that a disciple is even a committed follower of a great master! What type of commitment did those disciples who turned their back on Jesus have?

The connotation of the word in the book of Acts is distinctly different from its connotation in the Gospels. Unlike the Gospels, where the word meant learner, follower, or potentially adherent, the word "disciple" in the book of Acts now denoted someone who accepted the Christian faith and had become a believer in Jesus as Savior and Lord. With the Lord risen, and the apostles filled with the Holy Spirit, the invitation to repentance and to faith in the risen Lord was clearly given, so only those who believed were called disciples. It is as if the term evolved through time from being a description of someone who followed a teacher—be it the Lord Jesus or others—to being a description of someone who actually believed in Jesus as Savior and Lord.

This brief exposé brings out seven important observations:

1) The first observation is that the New Testament gospel writers used the word "disciple" somewhat loosely in describing those who followed Jesus. To them, the term meant different things at different times. That explains why John, in his gospel, seems imprecise and ambiguous as to the use of the term, though he states very explicitly that he wrote the gospel to lead his readers to believe in Jesus, the Son of God (see John 20:31).

2) We can also safely add that the gospel writers' definition of the word "disciple" was quite broad in terms of a disciple's commitment or the lack thereof, and in terms of the duration of such an individual's following of Jesus and learning from him.

3) The third observation is that the word "disciple" evolved and became better defined in the minds of the gospel writers over a spectrum of being simply a learner or follower to becoming a true believer. That progression is clear when we move from reading the Gospels to reading the book of Acts.

4) We also note that Luke, in Luke 6 and Luke 19, is the only gospel writer who describes throngs or crowds of people as being disciples. The other gospel writers only use that term in reference to individuals or to the twelve. Since we know that the gospel crowds were not committed believers in Jesus, we should also question how strongly committed were the crowds that Luke refers to in Acts. This is not to question their personal or communal faith in Christ, especially since those disciples had followed through by being baptized and joining the church in Jerusalem. What we do question is their level of commitment compared to the level of commitment that is expected in the life of a Christian disciple in our present understanding.

Based on the previous observation, we question the general notion of whether any crowd of Christians could be called disciples, especially as Luke uses the term in the book of Acts. We know that these crowds had accepted the faith. We also know that once they were scattered due to the persecution that began in Jerusalem, they were involved in evangelizing others. Yet, what we do not know is whether they were actually groomed or discipled and by whom. Here again, the general notion is that Luke also uses that term loosely even in the book of Acts. The two exceptions that stand out from that crowd are Stephen and Barnabas.

5) One other observation is that the process of discipleship, or discipling, has by definition two sides to it: the discipler and the disciple. The absence of one party automatically means that the process breaks down.

6) We also notice that the process of discipling is very limited in its scope. More often than not, it involves one or two disciples at one time but not too many more. Jesus was the obvious exception when he trained the twelve. As we have seen above, the apostles probably succeeded in discipling Stephen and Barnabas, but not too many more beyond them. Ananias discipled Saul, who, in turn, discipled Timothy and Luke, among other individuals.

7) The last and final observation is that there is no single process from the above-mentioned verses that is expounded enough to

give us a discipling blueprint, with the exception of the model that Jesus followed with the twelve. We only have bits and pieces of the methodology that others used. It follows that our best chance of learning both ends of this process—of first being better disciples of the Lord, and second, discipling others—should thus be based on how Jesus discipled the twelve as traced out in the four Gospels. That will be the discussion of the next chapter.

CHAPTER III

THE TWELVE: JESUS' MAIN FOCUS

Jesus was born in a Jewish home and in a Jewish culture. And while He did spend time outside his immediate habitat, as He did in Phoenicia or in Samaria, the better part of his travels was confined to his homeland and with His people. It was from within His people group that He picked all twelve disciples. There were no Samaritans among them, and obviously none was from a gentile background.

We do not know, and the New Testament does not explain in any detail, why the Lord limited his choice of disciples to His people group. We are left to discover and decide that ourselves, with each Bible student extrapolating certain insight or, at times, reading into the text his or her view. One of the more familiar passages that are used to shed light on that question is John 1:11, where we read that Jesus, "came to that which was His own."

Though it may be important to know why Jesus did not choose disciples from a non-Jewish background, and though it may be as important to know why He limited His choices to His people group, the more important and valid question is what He sought to do with those men that He chose.

We can assume with confidence that His personal expectations—regardless of what those expectations were and whether the twelve succeeded in meeting them—led Him in His decision to pick them all from a Jewish background. He knew what He was doing, and He knew why He was doing it.

We cannot say that much about the twelve. Our reading of the New Testament leaves us wondering how much the twelve knew or understood of His general mission and, as or more important, of what their role would be in it. We are also left wondering why they followed an unknown teacher, carrying an unknown agenda, and leading to an unknown destiny. What was it that led them to leave everything and follow Him?

By identifying with the group of twelve that He picked, Jesus automatically created a number of expectations in their minds. They expected Him to go into the synagogues with them on Saturdays. They expected Him to regard in high esteem Abraham, Moses, David, and the prophets. They expected Him to uphold the Law and other aspects of their shared religious heritage.

Their expectations of Him were not limited to religious observances and practices. They expected Jesus to follow traditionally accepted Jewish behaviors, whether in the way Jesus dressed, what He ate or did not eat, and the way He addressed non-Jews, especially the despised Samaritans. As important, they expected of Him certain normative historical attitudes, for example, with regard to their Roman occupiers. They most probably saw in Him someone who could begin to fulfill their national aspirations, possibly leading them in a revolt or war of liberation.

Little did it cross their minds that they would be personally challenged to shift their paradigms on a constant basis on one issue after another, be it their stand against Samaritan or gentile, toward the Jewish religious establishment of their day, or the Roman slave masters. Had they known this the first day they followed him, they may have decided differently.

Little did they know that they would personally be His main focus and that His whole strategy would stand or fall based on whether He succeeded in making them the men He wanted them to become. The following passages of Scripture and the comments that follow will help clarify and validate this point.

The Encounter with the Canaanite Woman

In chapter 15 of His gospel, verses 21 to 28, Matthew presents to us a very Jewish picture:

> Leaving that place, Jesus withdrew to the region of Tyre and Sidon. A Canaanite woman from that vicinity came to him, crying out, "Lord, Son of David, have mercy on me! My daughter is suffering terribly from demon-possession." Jesus did not answer a word. So his disciples came to him and urged him, "Send her away, for she keeps crying out after us." He answered, "I was sent only to the lost sheep of Israel." The woman came and knelt before him. "Lord, help me!" she said. He replied, "It is not right to take the children's bread and toss it to their dogs." "Yes, Lord," she said, "but even the dogs eat the crumbs that fall from their masters' table." Then Jesus answered, "Woman, you have great faith! Your request is granted." And her daughter was healed from that very hour.

The picture that Matthew paints above is Jewish through and through. We can all understand the backdrop to the attitude of the twelve. To them, as to their compatriots, this woman was as worthy of attention as dogs were. That was the Jewish view. Her skin color probably stood out. Her strange and strong accent as she cried out after the Lord to heal her demon-terrorized daughter sounded foreign and alien. Those two elements alone were enough to betray her.

To the twelve, this woman did not belong. They decided that neither she nor her daughter were worth the effort. They asked Jesus to send her away. It would have been a refreshing surprise had the twelve taken a different attitude and perspective. Instead, their request of the Lord only accentuates the Jewish national, historical position, and that is no surprise to the readers of this text. Sadly, their ultra-nationalist attitude took preference over the woman's spiritual needs.

This picture is also very disturbing. It is very disturbing because of the position that Jesus seems to take. It seems as if He shared the view of his disciples, almost acting like their mouthpiece or spokesperson. His first utterance was, "I was sent only to the lost sheep of Israel."

As we read and ponder these words, we are left with even more questions. First, it was not the woman who came into Jewish territory; it was Jesus and the Twelve who walked into Canaanite country. So, if Jesus was, "'sent only to the lost sheep of Israel,'" what business did He have taking His disciples into Canaan? The inhabitants of that region were mostly Canaanites not Jews!

Jesus did not wander by mistake into the region of Tyre and Sidon. He knew where He was going and where He was leading His disciples.

This is rejection pure and simple. Not only was this woman's own gentile society rejecting her because of her daughter's situation; now, even the person on whom she had set high hopes was also rejecting her, though not for the same reasons. If that were not enough, the Lord adds insult to injury by saying that "It is not right to take the children's bread and toss it to their dogs."

For a minute or two, the reader is left wondering whether Jesus had also inherited and was practicing the same ethnic-conscious Jewish attitude toward the gentiles as that of His household. Yet, before we pass judgment on Jesus, we need to look more closely not only at the words that he uttered but at their sequence and timing.

The exchange began with the woman addressing Jesus in person, asking Him to heal her daughter. Jesus heard her plea but remained silent. We do not know for how long He remained silent. Was He ignoring her? His silence can be interpreted a hundred different ways. One of those would be His indifference. On the surface, it can be assumed that He neither cared nor bothered to pay any attention to what was unfolding right around Him.

In the meantime, the woman continued to cry out loudly; to clamor. She did that long enough to get on the disciples' nerves and strike a chord at their inherited religious partiality toward non-Jews. Since Jesus did not take a stand, the disciples did. They also interpreted His silence possibly to mean that He had nothing to do with or for this woman. So, they demanded that He send her away. If Jesus ignored her, His followers wanted to dismiss her completely.

Did they read their Master's mind, or did they misread it? It was at this point that the Lord made his first comment about being only sent to the lost sheep of Israel. As we will note later, this was not the only time that the Lord borrowed this specific image.

The reader wonders in the light of that whether Jesus succumbed to peer pressure from His disciples. Would they disown Him if He differed from them? Would they turn their backs on Him and stop following Him?

If Jesus did not succumb to peer pressure, and if His words were not about saving face, why would He address the woman in those terms and send such a strong message of rejection? Unless, of course, Jesus was not addressing the woman at all. Unless He was addressing the twelve.

Having waited for His followers to express openly their negative feelings toward non-Jews, Jesus chose the right moment to say what was on their minds and not on His. He waited so their discriminatory attitudes and preconceived ideas would betray them.

The Canaanites did not call themselves dogs. The Jews called them dogs. They also treated them as dogs: unclean. They had divided the world into two camps. In the one was a small herd of sheep, namely the Jewish people. And in the other was a huge herd of dogs: everybody else. Jesus borrowed that image from the Jewish culture and dictionary, because He was addressing a Jewish culture: that of His disciples.

If Jesus had succumbed to peer pressure, He would not have responded to the need that this woman presented. He would not have praised the faith of this gentile woman in front of his disciples. If anything, Jesus seized the occasion, as He did in other contexts with other gentiles, to exhort His Jewish hearers, specifically His own disciples, to greater faith in Himself by openly citing and praising the faith example of a "pet dog." For if such "pet dogs" can exercise such great faith in Him, why could not His "sheep"?

So, who was Jesus really addressing with his two comments? His disciples qualify better than the Canaanite woman. They were his main audience. It was them who He was turning into disciples, not the woman. It was them He was molding and shaping to become more like Himself, the Master. His trip to Tyre and Sidon, which was Phoenician territory, was a divine appointment for the woman, an appointment that He was not going to miss. But it was a practical hands-on lesson for his followers, which the Lord meant to use in his efforts to shape them. He made that road trip as much for His disciples as it was for this woman.

Matthew does not tell us how the disciples reacted after the event. Did their faith in Him increase after that? Were they willing, teachable, and humble enough to take a lesson from a "pet dog's" faith?

I can imagine that in their walk back to Galilee, they had some interesting material to discuss. The fact is that Matthew himself was so marked by what he witnessed that he recorded it in His account of the gospel, which many commentators believe was mostly written to a Jewish audience. So, in as much as Matthew himself was shaped and molded by the things he watched His Master do, he was seeking to see the same in his fellow Jews. The same can be said of Peter, who had John Mark write his account of the gospel, since he, too, recorded it in his account of the gospel.

The effect on the twelve must have been immense! But that is to be expected, since Jesus was mainly in the process of turning them into disciples, and he used every occasion to achieve that noble and most important objective.

The general reader of the New Testament is flabbergasted by the wisdom, the power, the love, and the sacrifice of the Lord, as Matthew,

Mark, Luke, and John tell His story. Bible students are no less amazed as they dig deeper into the meaning of all that they read. Yet, for all the hours spent on reading and studying, many among us often miss that very important and focal point. It is the fact that in as much as the Lord was teaching and performing miracles, reaching out and touching men, women, and children, his own disciples were his first audience. They were His main focus.

This would immediately explain the enormous amount of time that He spent with them compared with the much less amount of time He was with the crowds. And even during those times that He was with the crowds, the twelve were there with Him. He talked and walked with them. He ate and slept with them. He was with them from the minute He called them to follow Him until He hung on the cross.

The encounter with the Canaanite woman is only one of many examples by which the Lord tempered, softened, changed, and finally prepared His first followers. All those steps were part of the process of disciple-making that He had undertaken with them.

THE ENCOUNTER WITH THE CROWDS

Mark, in his gospel, brings out the same truth when he recounts how the Lord addressed the crowd that had gathered around him and presented to them the parable of the sower. We read in Mark 4:1-12:

> Again Jesus began to teach by the lake. The crowd that gathered around him was so large that he got into a boat and sat in it out on the lake, while all the people were along the shore at the water's edge. He taught them many things by parables, and in his teaching said: "Listen! A farmer went out to sow his seed. As he was scattering the seed, some fell along the path, and the birds came and ate it up. Some fell on rocky places, where it did not have much soil. It sprang up quickly, because the soil was shallow. But when the sun came up, the plants were scorched, and they withered because they had no root. Other seed fell among thorns, which grew up and choked the plants, so that they did

not bear grain. Still other seed fell on good soil. It came up, grew and produced a crop, multiplying thirty, sixty, or even a hundred times."

Then Jesus said, "He who has ears to hear, let him hear." When he was alone, the Twelve and the others around him asked him about the parables. He told them, "The secret of the kingdom of God has been given to you. But to those on the outside everything is said in parables so that, "'they may be ever seeing but never perceiving, and ever hearing but never understanding; otherwise they might turn and be forgiven!'"

Mark is clear in stating that the Lord did not explain that parable to the crowd to whom, at least on the surface, He seemed to be addressing it. We wonder why the Lord would teach the crowd something they were not meant to understand or about which they were not expected to even ask. Who was He addressing? Was it really the crowd? Or was it His disciples?

Mark answered these last two questions in verse 11. His answer is very significant to our study. He quoted Jesus saying, "'The secret of the kingdom of God has been given to you. But to those on the outside everything is said in parables'" (Mark 4:11). Jesus then went on to explain the meaning behind the symbols of that parable.

Jesus was obviously addressing not the crowds that had gathered, though those did hear him, too. He was in reality addressing the twelve. They were the first audience.

THE TWELVE ON THEIR FIRST MISSION

To clarify this point further, we turn back to the gospel according to Matthew and chapter 10, where the twelve were sent on their first mission. They were given authority to drive out evil spirits. They were granted power to heal every disease and every sickness. And yet, Jesus confounds us with the following instruction. He said to them, "'Do not go among the Gentiles or enter any town of the Samaritans. Go rather to the lost sheep of Israel'" (Matthew 10:5-6). This is the same terminology that is quoted in Matthew 15, above.

While it may be true that Matthew wrote his gospel to a mainly Jewish audience, he could not be accused of inserting Jewish prejudices to appease that audience. So, why would Jesus forbid the twelve from meeting the spiritual and physical needs of the Gentiles and the Samaritans, when He reached out to a Samaritan woman among many other non-Jews? Why would He deny his followers doing things that He did Himself? Is not a teacher expected to set an example by the choices and the decisions he or she makes?

One answer advanced by many an expositor and teacher is that the primary mission of the Lord was to reach His own. To help validate that opinion, many turn to the gospel of John (John 1:11), where we read of Jesus, "He came to that which was his own, but his own did not receive him." This is the same verse that many use in their attempts to understand and even justify some of the positions and statements that the Lord made, such as His comments to the Canaanite woman, or in this specific case, His marching orders to the twelve on their first mission.

If that answer were correct, then neither the Samaritans nor the Gentiles were part of the original plan and mission of Jesus. These would be afterthoughts, or add-ons, used for expediency so that His mission to planet Earth would not be perceived as having completely failed. Understood in that way, it would only make sense for Jesus to send out His disciples on a mission that has the exact same parameters, therefore, the verses in Matthew 10. This is not the place to discuss the validity of such an opinion or position or discredit its proponents. I have to leave that discussion until another time and another book. Yet, in my opinion, there could be two more plausible answers, and here they are.

The first plausible answer is that the Samaritans, for one, were not ready to receive a Jew or a Jewish crowd in their midst. Suffice to look at the time when a Jewish town denied Jesus and His men from even going through their town. Luke describes such a scene in his gospel, 9:51-56. Here is how it reads.

> As the time approached for him to be taken up to heaven, Jesus resolutely set out for Jerusalem. And he sent messengers on ahead, who went into a Samaritan village to get things ready for him; but the people there did not welcome him, because he was heading for Jerusalem. When the disciples James and John saw this, they asked, "Lord, do you want us to call fire down from heaven to destroy them[b]?" But Jesus turned and rebuked them. Then he and his disciples went to another village.

If the Samaritans, according to the text above, were not willing to allow them passage, how much less would they have harkened to a message carried to them by Jews, who traditionally looked down on them. If anything, such a message would smell of a holier-than-thou attitude and would be categorically rejected, along with its Jewish bearers.

The other side of the same coin presents the second plausible answer. Judging by their background, outlook, and general perspective, the twelve were not yet ready to be involved in a mission, any mission, to non-Jews. Their cultural, ethnic, and religious biases were still stronger than any sympathy toward the "other" that they may have developed walking with their Master. We have in the Bible text just quoted the reaction of James and John. How, therefore, could Jesus entrust to unregenerated individuals, who had yet to receive the transforming power of the Holy Spirit, such a task? One would think that given the time, the disciples would have finally changed and developed a different mind-set. One would think that the love of Jesus toward the Samaritans would have automatically filtered down to the twelve. But the fact is that such expectations could not be further from the truth.

Jesus spent three and a half years with them, almost to the exclusion of everyone else. They had Him all to themselves to learn from and to emulate. Not only that, ten days after His ascension, He sent the Holy Spirit in a marvelous outpouring, baptizing them as He promised with fire that normally should have consumed every little trace of their old nature. And yet, to our chagrin, as we walk in their tracks, we continue to see elements in them that should have long disappeared.

That may sound harsh and unjust. Yet, the facts speak for themselves. To help prove this point, we take a brief detour, looking more closely at the life of Peter, after which we will go back to our study.

PETER'S ROOFTOP EXPERIENCE

In Acts 10, we read of an interesting vision that Peter, of all the twelve, experienced. Here is how Luke described it. We pick up the story after Cornelius, a gentile Roman centurion, sent two of his servants and one soldier to the city of Joppa to fetch Peter (Acts 10:9-23).

> About noon the following day as they were on their journey and approaching the city, Peter went up on the roof to pray. He became hungry and wanted something to eat, and while the meal was being prepared, he fell into a trance. He saw heaven opened and something like a large sheet being let down to earth by its four corners. It contained all kinds of four-footed animals, as well as reptiles of the earth and birds of the air. Then a voice told him, "Get up, Peter. Kill and eat."
>
> "Surely not, Lord!" Peter replied. "I have never eaten anything impure or unclean." The voice spoke to him a second time, "Do not call anything impure that God has made clean." This happened three times, and immediately the sheet was taken back to heaven.
>
> While Peter was wondering about the meaning of the vision, the men sent by Cornelius found out where Simon's house was and stopped at the gate. They called out, asking if Simon who was known as Peter was staying there.
>
> While Peter was still thinking about the vision, the Spirit said to him, "Simon, three men are looking for you. So get up and go downstairs. Do not hesitate to go with them, for I have sent them."
>
> Peter went down and said to the men, "I'm the one you're looking for. Why have you come?" The men replied, "We have come from

Cornelius the centurion. He is a righteous and God-fearing man, who is respected by all the Jewish people. A holy angel told him to have you come to his house so that he could hear what you have to say." Then Peter invited the men into the house to be his guests.

Peter recognized the Lord's voice. He had heard it hundreds of times before, while the Lord was there in the flesh with them. Judging by his answer, Peter probably thought the Lord was testing him. He had never eaten anything impure or unclean. So, why would the Lord ask him to do that now?

The Lord corrected his understanding, telling him not to call anything impure that God had made clean. Peter was not quite convinced. He stubbornly refused to follow what He was being told. But the Lord did not give up. It became obvious that some lessons are harder to penetrate and are worth repeating a second and a third time. Rather, some attitudes and preconceived ideas are harder to break and, therefore, dictate seconds and thirds. So, the Lord gave his orders to Peter three consecutive times.

If Peter was initially stubborn, now he was confused. He did not quite know what to make out of that vision. What was the Lord asking him to do, why did that require a vision, and why did the Lord repeat Himself three times? He may not have known the answers to these questions. But one thing he knew: the Lord was about to teach him a very important lesson, and He wanted to make sure Peter got it; therefore, the repeats.

While still wondering about the meaning of what he saw, the three men sent by Cornelius showed up at the house where Peter was staying. One more time the Lord had to intervene personally and speak to Peter, telling him to go with these gentile men.

Once in the centurion's home, Peter made the following introduction: "You are well aware that it is against our law for a Jew to associate with a Gentile or visit him. But God has shown me that I should not call any man impure or unclean. So when I was sent for, I came without raising any objection" (Acts 10:28-29).

Peter's personal introduction presents a good number of interesting aspects, revealing admissions, and some open questions. Let me start with the questions.

Who was Peter addressing? If he was addressing Cornelius, why did he feel compelled to explain why he was coming into his home, especially since Cornelius had sent for him and was expecting him? By the sound of it, it seems that Peter was attempting to justify his act of coming into the home of a gentile. But then, who was he trying to justify that to and before? Was it to God or was it to himself? We learn from the story that several brothers from the city of Joppa—believers of Jewish background—accompanied Peter. See Acts 10:23. Was Peter seeking to justify himself before them? Or maybe he was already picturing himself, standing before the church council in Jerusalem and answering to them. If so, those same Jewish men who accompanied him from Joppa would serve as valid witnesses of what had actually happened and potentially defend Peter before the Jerusalem council, which was made up of Jewish-background believers.

As we move beyond the questions, we observe that Peter continued to consider himself a Jew, therefore following the directives of the Law of Moses in disassociating himself from gentile company. He was still accountable to that Law. His loyalty had not changed. It took direct intervention from heaven to begin to break the limitations the Law placed on his life.

Peter also admitted that it took divine intervention to make him come, though he forgoes the fact that God had to repeat Himself three times for him to do it, and on top of it, to speak to him again to make him come. Were it not for divine intervention, Peter would have declined the invitation from Cornelius and would still be, to this day, in Joppa, among his people.

In light of the above, we are left to wonder in what ways Peter changed. He, along with James and John, received very special attention from the Lord, who had spent the most time with them. And of all the twelve, it was Peter who delivered the famous sermon on the day of Pentecost. He was the leading apostle to whom the Lord gave the keys to the Kingdom, opening the way for Jews, Samaritans, and gentiles to enter therein.

Yet, as is obvious, some things had not changed at all. Peter was still dealing with the pure and impure, the clean and the unclean, and not just with animals. He was still considering non-Jews unworthy of his association, as he admitted himself. His Jewish biases were quite deep-seated, and those shackles would prove very hard to break.

Paul's Issue with Peter

We read of another incident where Peter's personal challenges surfaced again. This time, it was in the city of Antioch. The details of that are recorded for us in Paul's letter to the Galatians (Galatians 2:11-14).

> When Peter came to Antioch, I opposed him to his face, because he was clearly in the wrong. Before certain men came from James, he used to eat with the Gentiles. But when they arrived, he began to draw back and separate himself from the Gentiles because he was afraid of those who belonged to the circumcision group. The other Jews joined him in his hypocrisy, so that by their hypocrisy even Barnabas was led astray. When I saw that they were not acting in line with the truth of the gospel, I said to Peter in front of them all, "You are a Jew, yet you live like a Gentile and not like a Jew. How is it, then, that you force Gentiles to follow Jewish customs?

Peter's hypocrisy was too much for Paul to accept or allow. He rebuked and accused him of acting against the spirit of the Gospel, adding a very condemning rhetoric question: "How is it, then, that you force Gentiles to follow Jewish customs?"

Peter was obviously his own prisoner. At a time when he should have long been free of his own Jewish customs, he was allowing himself to continue to be chained to them. Furthermore, he was seeking to impose them on believers from a non-Jewish background. His Jewish sentiments and attachments were not going to go away anytime soon.

Back to the twelve's first mission, where the Lord sent His disciples with the following directive: "'Do not go among the Gentiles or enter any town of the Samaritans. Go rather to the lost sheep of Israel'" (Matthew 10:5-6).

We can safely assume that the Jewish social, cultural, and religious attitudes toward non-Jews were not Peter's problem alone. His fellow disciples shared the same challenges to a lesser or greater degree. It was no wonder, therefore, that the Lord would limit their first mission to only Jews. Had it been otherwise, they would have probably caused more harm than good: more offense than blessing. Jesus purely and simply avoided that. There was still a lot of role modeling for Him to do before and with them.

The general Gospel reader wonders why Jesus spent three short years only ministering, when He could have stayed ten times that long and done ten times as much good. One answer is that His reason for coming was not necessarily to do as much good Himself as possible. Rather, it was to choose and prepare men and women who would do that in the same way He did; hence, His emphasis in choosing and training disciples. With that thought in mind, it becomes of utmost importance at every encounter, with every miracle, and at the utterance of every teaching that the Lord gave for us to ask such questions as these: What was it that Jesus meant to teach His disciples through this miracle, encounter, or utterance? What change was He seeking to see in them? How did this or that miracle prepare them for their future mission?

THE ENCOUNTER WITH THE DEMON-POSSESSED

To further clarify, we will take up the following example. Mark, as does Matthew and Luke, records one eventful crossing of the lake that Jesus asked His disciples to undertake. Here is Mark's rendering of it, according to his gospel (Mark 4:35-5:20):

> That day when evening came, he said to his disciples, "Let us go over to the other side." Leaving the crowd behind, they took him

along, just as he was, in the boat. There were also other boats with him. A furious squall came up, and the waves broke over the boat, so that it was nearly swamped. Jesus was in the stern, sleeping on a cushion. The disciples woke him and said to him, "Teacher, don't you care if we drown?"

He got up, rebuked the wind and said to the waves, "Quiet! Be still!" Then the wind died down and it was completely calm. He said to his disciples, "Why are you so afraid? Do you still have no faith?" They were terrified and asked each other, "Who is this? Even the wind and the waves obey him!" They went across the lake to the region of the Gerasenes. When Jesus got out of the boat, a man with an evil spirit came from the tombs to meet him. This man lived in the tombs, and no one could bind him any more, not even with a chain. For he had often been chained hand and foot, but he tore the chains apart and broke the irons on his feet. No one was strong enough to subdue him. Night and day among the tombs and in the hills he would cry out and cut himself with stones.

When he saw Jesus from a distance, he ran and fell on his knees in front of him. He shouted at the top of his voice, "What do you want with me, Jesus, Son of the Most High God? Swear to God that you won't torture me!" For Jesus had said to him, "Come out of this man, you evil spirit!"

Then Jesus asked him, "What is your name?" "My name is Legion," he replied, "for we are many." And he begged Jesus again and again not to send them out of the area. A large herd of pigs was feeding on the nearby hillside. The demons begged Jesus, "Send us among the pigs; allow us to go into them." He gave them permission, and the evil spirits came out and went into the pigs. The herd, about two thousand in number, rushed down the steep bank into the lake and were drowned.

Those tending the pigs ran off and reported this in the town and countryside, and the people went out to see what had happened. When they came to Jesus, they saw the man who had been possessed by the legion of demons, sitting there, dressed and in his right mind; and they were afraid. Those who had seen it told the people what had happened to the demon-possessed man—and told about the pigs as well. Then the people began to plead with Jesus to leave their region.

As Jesus was getting into the boat, the man who had been demon-possessed begged to go with him. Jesus did not let him, but said, "Go home to your family and tell them how much the Lord has done for you, and how he has had mercy on you." So the man went away and began to tell in the Decapolis how much Jesus had done for him. And all the people were amazed.

If, in fact, the twelve were the priority audience of Jesus, as we suggested previously, we can now ask the following questions: What was Jesus trying to teach His disciples, whether on their way to the other side of the lake, by calming the storm, or by any other aspect of the whole event? What change was He seeking to see in them? How did this event or encounter prepare them for their future mission?

For one, the twelve received another hint as to the true identity of their Master. They watched Him rule over nature in ways that only their ancestors had witnessed once before, when God ripped the Red Sea in two and allowed His people to go through unharmed. Their minds raced back to that event, as they stood bedazzled by the authority that their Master demonstrated. Yet, rather than fall on their knees, all they could muster was a question: who is this?

The other side of the lake, where Jesus led them—namely the southeastern shore of Lake Galilee—was a region inhabited by a mixed pagan people who, as the text clearly affirms, made their living herding pigs. It was not a region any of the disciples would have chosen to go to if he had a say in this. And it was not the waves that sent them there, either. So, why would Jesus order his disciples to go there with Him? Was it to look for one sick demon-possessed pagan? Just one! Was He here also trying to model His message before His disciples with His life, his choices, his decisions, and His values? Assuredly, Jesus was sending a message that even for one sick person,

He will risk His own life, and they should be willing to do the same. Could this serve as a reminder for them when He did not only risk but literally gave His life on the cross to save sin-sick people? Did He not cross the heavens and come down to earth to do just that? Was the crossing of the lake a preview of a more important fact they would understand later?

James and John, Peter and Andrew were by trade fishermen, and their place of work was this very lake. They had crisscrossed this lake many times before. But it is doubtful that they ever approached the southeastern side of it. They knew better. They who had been raised on the strict Jewish faith and tradition were not going to dehumanize themselves by going to pagan country, not even if the fish at that side was plentiful. Crossing the aisle to meet the other was not in the nature of these men. And definitely not crossing the aisle when the "other" is a demon-possessed pagan. Was Jesus hoping to see them discard some of their prejudices against non-Jews to the point of risking their lives in an attempt to save them?

Jesus faced multiple challenges on every side. On the one, He had the Sanhedrin, the Jewish religious authority with which to deal. On another, He had the Roman rulers, who wanted peace at any cost, even if it meant the death of an innocent person. Then, He obviously had the crowds: the men, women, and children who came to Him for healing, for bread, and for all types of other needs. Yet, his biggest challenge was taking a group of opinionated, power-greedy, faithless, prejudiced, and weak individuals and turning them into a powerhouse in His name. The wind He could calm with a word, and the dead he could raise with a touch, but His disciples needed three full years of constant prodding, teaching, and counseling before He could entrust them to do what He did.

CHAPTER IV

JESUS' MODEL OF DISCIPLESHIP

One of the striking observations that the reader of the New Testament comes across is the following: how come, in their three-plus years of living with Jesus, only one of the twelve disciples ever asked to learn anything? According to Luke's gospel, after watching Jesus pray, one of the disciples went to Him and requested of Him, saying, "Lord, teach us how to pray just as John taught his disciples" (Luke 11:1).

It may well be that the one disciple who spoke up was either hiding behind the others when he used the plural pronoun "us," or he was truthfully asking on behalf of the others. But even then, did he, or did they, not find anything else they could ask to learn from their Master? How come no one of them asked Jesus to learn how to fast or, better still, how to preach or how to interpret Scripture or any one aspect from the life of the Master? Was praying such a hard thing to learn that someone had to ask to be taught how to do it? Or is there another secret to this puzzling question?

Bible students and general readers could possibly find half a dozen answers to this question, and possibly as many reasons for that question to be asked. Today, we are glad someone asked. Or are we? For while we all value the Lord's Prayer and hundreds of millions have learned it by heart in one or more languages, and millions more pray it every day, it is quite possible that this same prayer has become a ritual so routine that many do not contemplate its words as they pray it. It has sadly replaced one's personal expressions of worship and supplication.

Moreover, it is striking that as we move from the Gospels into the book of Acts, Luke records no testimony as to the apostles or their disciples ever using that prayer or teaching others to pray it.

It is also worth noting that the descriptive term "how" is not explicit in the Greek original. The text *"didaxon hemas proseuchesthai"* is best rendered "teach us to be praying." The "how" is only implied. And if such inference is valid, we find that, indeed, Jesus did not answer the disciple's question. The "how" refers to methods and ways. The "what" would refer to content. The disciple was probably more interested in comparing the ritualistic prayers that he had learned and possibly practiced to what he and his colleagues saw the Master do. Yet, Jesus did not get caught in that quandary. He had not come to replace one method of prayer with another. So, He used the occasion of this request to teach His disciples not "how" to pray, but "what" to pray. To Jesus, the important elements are not whether we pray kneeling or standing, whether we lift our hands, or if we lift our eyes. What matters is that our hearts be lifted before the Father.

In my estimation, the disciple's request was veiled, almost an excuse that hid the disciple's or disciples' challenge in having a similar prayer life to the one the Master demonstrated before them. In that sense, the disciple was not really looking for an answer. And here is why. There was no need to even make that one request, since Jesus had modeled his teaching with his life and, most especially, had modeled his prayer life with a life of prayer.

To many among us, disciple-making is a course of study. It is classes, books, and homework. It is tests, certificates, and graduation. It is a weekly or bi-weekly meeting that we as mentors have with our disciple, or as disciples with our teacher and mentor, when we go over the next chapter or the next book or booklet. But that obviously was not the methodology that Jesus used in preparing His disciples. Seen in this way, the one request made by the one disciple becomes not striking because of its rarity but because of its appearance in the text. In other words, what need was there to ask to learn how to pray when that disciple had a whole life of prayer that Jesus lived out before him?

It is a whole lot easier to teach someone a course on how to read the Bible than to spend day after day with him or her reading the Bible. It is a whole lot easier to teach someone a course on prayer than to spend hours day after day praying with him or her. In short, one cannot begin to compare the difference in investment of oneself, whether in one's time or in energy. But the investment of oneself in simply teaching a course, even if that were on a daily basis, and in living that course and actualizing it before one's disciple or disciples is huge. The stakes are much higher, and the risks are greater.

But then, this is exactly what Jesus did as He surrounded Himself with those twelve men. For three long years, day in and day out, Jesus lived out every aspect of what He expected His disciples to become. The four Gospels are testimonies to that model of disciple-making. The method of Jesus in disciple-making was not through question-and-answer sessions. This is why this one instance and one request stand out. His life was to be the course work to emulate and follow.

We know that the Jewish background of the twelve influenced many if not most of their religious, political, and social perspectives and attitudes. One example within the religious realm would be their perspective on the Law of Moses, whether it is the keeping of the Sabbath or other aspects of that Law. In the political arena, their background would have colored their views and attitudes toward the Roman occupier who ruled them. Among the socioreligious aspects would be their relationship to the Samaritans and the long history of that relationship.

Jesus was not born into a religious void, nor did he choose His disciples from a nondescript religious background. All twelve were Jewish men through and through. Being born Jewish Himself, Jesus knew firsthand the various influences that had shaped the disciples' thinking, outlook, and attitudes.

And add to the mix, then, their individual differences; their personal, family, and social backgrounds; their egos and personal traits, whether inherited or acquired; their likes and dislikes; and their personal trades and skills. Piercing through all this came the Lord's personal call to each of them to follow him. Time was not on the Lord's side. He could not go back and straighten out whatever negative family or other acquired influences they had. He also could not work with each of these men singly. Plus, these were obviously adult men, already set in their ways, with at least one married man, namely Peter, and possibly others. The following are a few examples from the life of the Lord in his methodology of turning His followers into His disciples.

THE MOSAIC LAW AND INFECTIOUS DISEASES

The book of Leviticus outlines procedures to help the priest determine if someone has a leprous disease. When such is the case, the priest had very strict rules to enforce on such an infected individual. Leviticus 13:45-46 sums up the rules as follows:

> The person with such an infectious disease must wear torn clothes, let his hair be unkempt, cover the lower part of his face and cry out, "Unclean! Unclean!" As long as he has the infection he remains unclean. He must live alone; he must live outside the camp.

The above rules were very clearly laid out, with their main objective to control the disease. Leprosy was contagious, as were some other skin diseases. The only person qualified to call the infected individual healed or clean was the priest, which explains the order that Jesus gave to the leper in Matthew 8:1-4, where we read:

> When he came down from the mountainside, large crowds followed him. A man with leprosy came and knelt before him and said, "Lord, if you are willing, you can make me clean." Jesus reached out his hand and touched the man. "I am willing," he said. "Be clean!" Immediately he was cured of his leprosy. Then Jesus said to him, "See that you don't tell anyone. But go, show

yourself to the priest and offer the gift Moses commanded, as a testimony to them."

Jesus had no reason to break the Law of Moses, and He did not. What He did break was the erroneous interpretation of the Law, which made it superior to what served the interests of the Kingdom. As a rule, every time the Lord healed a leprous person, He would order the person to follow the letter of the Law, show himself or herself to the priest, and offer the gift as prescribed by the Law.

Matthew does not tell us whether this leper came into town at a time when he should have stayed outside the camp, or whether Jesus purposefully went outside the camp to meet this leper. But in either case, the Law does specify that until a leper is declared cured by the priest, he should not come in contact with anyone for fear of contaminating that person.

It is very doubtful that the disciples did not know the regulations governing leprous people. So, how did they put together the two sides of this encounter: on the one hand, Jesus touching a leprous person, seemingly in defiance of the Law, and on the other, Jesus following the letter of the Law by sending him directly to a priest? If nothing else, that surely confused them.

Jesus had three years to reveal gradually to His disciples what He called in Matthew 13:11, "the knowledge of the secrets of the Kingdom of heaven." One of those secrets Jesus would reveal in Matthew 9:13, when He said, quoting from Hosea 6:6, "'I desire mercy, not sacrifice!'" Those open secrets would help clear any confusion on the part of His disciples, and sometimes others too, as well as bridge their old, literal understanding of the Mosaic Law with the new spiritual insight and truth they gained from their Master.

Over time, the disciples probably understood that by touching the leper, Jesus was taking on Himself his disease. That touch allowed the disease to be removed from the leper onto Jesus and, thus, made the leper whole again. The promises in the book of Isaiah 53:4-5 were to be literally fulfilled. Matthew would refer to that in His gospel in 8:17, where he states, "This was to fulfill what was spoken through the prophet Isaiah: 'He took up our infirmities and carried our diseases.'"

The Jewish Nation and the Roman Occupiers

In the Sermon on the Mount in Matthew, chapters 5-7, the Lord covers a multitude of important Kingdom principles. Most of these principles had new spiritual dimensions, both to the crowd in general and to the disciples. Though all were spiritual in nature, a number of verses, and most especially the beginning verses of that sermon, seem to have carried political undertones. Here is how Matthew records these first few verses.

"Blessed are the poor in spirit, for theirs is the kingdom of heaven. Blessed are those who mourn, for they will be comforted.

Blessed are the meek, for they will inherit the earth. Blessed are those who hunger and thirst for righteousness, for they will be filled. Blessed are the merciful, for they will be shown mercy. Blessed are the pure in heart, for they will see God. Blessed are the peacemakers, for they will be called sons of God. Blessed are those who are persecuted because of righteousness, for theirs is the kingdom of heaven. Blessed are you when people insult you, persecute you and falsely say all kinds of evil against you because of me. Rejoice and be glad, because great is your reward in heaven, for in the same way they persecuted the prophets who were before you."

Contrary to all Jewish expectations, including those of His disciples, the Lord laid down new principles for attaining the Kingdom of God. These had absolutely nothing to do with the general Jewish outlook, which had its eyes fixed on restoring the Jewish national and ethnic identity, and getting rid of the Roman occupier. To Jesus, the Kingdom is not established by rising up in arms against the occupier, as was frequent in the history of the Jews. To Him, the true conquerors are those who are poor in spirit, those who mourn, the meek, the merciful, the peacemakers, and even those who suffer under persecution. The poor in spirit, according to Him, are the dwellers of the Kingdom, and the meek will inherit the earth!

This message was understandably very difficult to accept, much more so than any other teaching relating to the Kingdom. If anything, his hearers wanted to hear, "liberation theology," not, "surrender theology." It was hard enough to be salt and light at a time when the history of the Jewish nation was anything but that. It was hard enough to introduce a new interpretation of the Law of Moses, which to the Jews was sacred. It was hard enough to make them cross the aisle and meet the Samaritans halfway. Yet, for Jesus to send what sounded like a message of capitulation to the Romans was completely unacceptable. It was reminiscent of Jeremiah's message of capitulation to the Babylonians, which in his days was interpreted as treason, and for which he paid dearly.

In short, these new principles were completely foreign to the ears of the hearers. If anything, they smelled of treason. The Jews were suffering under the pagan Roman occupation. God could not side with the Romans against His own people. The promises He made to His people fill the pages of the Old Testament. Jesus could not be asking His hearers to give in to the Romans, give up their dream of independence, and turn the other cheek. As it turned out, He was. Later in that sermon, He would spell out some of those things in much clearer terms. "'Love your enemies,'" He would say, "'and pray for those who persecute you'" (Matthew 5:44). The enemies of the Jews were not the Samaritans. Those who persecuted the Jews were not the Phoenicians. They were the Romans. The words of Jesus had no other possible interpretation to His hearers except to, "Love the Romans!" That was His message. That was the message they heard.

On today's platforms and in today's church pulpits, these verses mostly take on a spiritual dimension without the historical background and the political baggage that come with them. One would almost have to travel to a church in the Middle East to sense the fullness of how loaded and how explosive such verses were back in those days. It is like asking a native of Israel today to love Palestinians, Syrians, or

Iranians. It is like asking Palestinians, other Arabs, and Muslims to accept and love Israelis.

On top of all this, John the Baptist, and more fully, Jesus came proclaiming the advent of the Kingdom. Matthew records scores of times when the Lord made mention of that word. How did that fall on the ears of the disciples? Did that help them understand the spiritual nature of the message that He announced, or did it only help boost their political ambitions and aspirations for the establishment of a new earthly kingdom? This, after all, was a term that Jesus borrowed from the world of politics, to which he added a heavenly dimension. That dimension was mostly incomprehensible for the disciples.

So, what chances of success could Jesus have? What chance could He have of changing not only the crowds' political outlook and align it with His teaching on the Kingdom but, more important, what chance of changing the outlook of His disciples? How far would He go to make that happen? Would He stop at conveying His strong message simply by word of mouth, or would He go further? In other words, how far in His disciple-making method was the Lord willing to go?

JEWISH-SAMARITAN RELATIONS

The Jews harbored nothing but disdain toward the Samaritans. They made every effort to avoid coming in contact with them; so much so, that to travel from Galilee to Judea, the Jews normally went all the way down to the Jordan valley, via Jericho, and then climbed back up to Jerusalem. The shorter route would take them via Samaria, something they chose not to do. The twelve were very much part of that tradition. Jesus witnessed that firsthand.

So, how did Jesus deal with this issue in the life of His disciples? How did He enlarge their horizon? There was never a more eloquent speaker, which means it would have made sense for Him to sit them before the disciples and lecture them. He was also the best storyteller, which means He could have told them a story or a parable and conveyed His message. While both means are good and noble, and while He did use both, his model and method of disciple-making went well beyond that. John chapter 4 provides an excellent example.

The Pharisees heard that Jesus was gaining and baptizing more disciples than John, although in fact it was not Jesus who baptized, but his disciples. When the Lord learned of this, he left Judea and went back once more to Galilee. Now he had to go through Samaria. So he came to a town in Samaria called Sychar, near the plot of ground Jacob had given to his son Joseph. Jacob's well was there, and Jesus, tired as he was from the journey, sat down by the well. It was about the sixth hour.

When a Samaritan woman came to draw water, Jesus said to her, "Will you give me a drink?" (His disciples had gone into the town to buy food.) The Samaritan woman said to him, "You are a Jew and I am a Samaritan woman. How can you ask me for a drink?" (For Jews do not associate with Samaritans.)

Jesus answered her, "If you knew the gift of God and who it is that asks you for a drink, you would have asked him and he would have given you living water." "Sir," the woman said, "you have nothing to draw with and the well is deep. Where can you get this living water? Are you greater than our father Jacob, who gave us the well and drank from it himself, as did also his sons and his flocks and herds?" Jesus answered, "Everyone who drinks this water will be thirsty again, but whoever drinks the water I give him will never thirst. Indeed, the water I give him will become in him a spring of water welling up to eternal life."

The woman said to him, "Sir, give me this water so that I won't get thirsty and have to keep coming here to draw water." He told her, "Go, call your husband and come back." "I have no husband," she replied. Jesus said to her, "You are right when you say you have no husband. The fact is, you have had five husbands, and the man you now have is not your husband. What you have just said is quite true." "Sir," the woman said, "I can see that you are a prophet. Our fathers worshiped on this mountain, but you Jews claim that the place where we must worship is in Jerusalem."

Jesus declared, "Believe me, woman, a time is coming when you will worship the Father neither on this mountain nor in Jerusalem. You Samaritans worship what you do not know; we worship what we do know, for salvation is from the Jews. Yet a time is coming and has now come when the true worshipers will worship the Father in spirit and truth, for they are the kind of worshipers the Father seeks. God is spirit, and his worshipers must worship in spirit and in truth."

The woman said, "I know that Messiah" (called Christ) "is coming. When he comes, he will explain everything to us." Then Jesus declared, "I who speak to you am he." Just then his disciples returned and were surprised to find him talking with a woman. But no one asked, "What do you want?" or "Why are you talking with her?"

John states that Jesus had to go through Samaria on his way from Judea to Galilee. We wonder why, when He could have chosen to go the roundabout way, like most of His compatriots. He did not consult with His disciples; he made the decision. Chances are that had He consulted with them, they would have unanimously objected to the idea. The Scriptures do provide other instances where the Lord did go the roundabout way. One such instance resulted in the encounter He had with Zaccheus in the city of Jericho. Or should we say that His Divine appointment with Zaccheus demanded that He go the roundabout way, probably in the same way that His Divine appointment with the unnamed Samaritan woman also demanded that He go through Samaria—thus the use of the phrase, "had to go," that we find in this text (John 4:4)?

Tired and thirsty from the journey, Jesus sat to rest at Jacob's well, and lo and behold, He initiates a discussion with a Samaritan woman who came to draw water. Jesus was still in the heat of it when the disciples showed up. John, the gospel writer and one of the twelve, contented himself by noting that he, along with the others, "were *surprised* to find Him talking with a woman" (italics mine) (John 4:27).

"Surprised" is a mild term to use in this context. In talking with a Samaritan woman, Jesus was literally shattering His disciples' worldview. He was breaking not one but two strong Jewish traditions, crossing two aisles at the same time—the gender aisle and the ethnicity aisle—both taboo in the minds of the twelve. Yet, what better example to set before them than to live out His Godly principles? Rather than make them sit down for Him to lecture them while they took notes, and rather than asking them to do things completely against their nature and only gain their disapproval, Jesus actualized His message. He gave it flesh and blood. His own! He became not the messenger. He became the message.

The twelve had gone to buy food. Yet, Jesus did not partake of it. His was a more important mission, even at the expense of remaining hungry and possibly thirsty. What message was He sending to His disciples? What was He trying to change in them?

Major challenges are presented when trying to reconcile His commission to the twelve in Matthew 10, where He said, "'Do not go among the Gentiles or enter any town of the Samaritans. Go rather to the lost sheep of Israel,'" with what He said in John 4:34: "'My food,' said Jesus, 'is to do the will of him who sent Me and to finish his work.'" How could He order the disciples to avoid bringing the good news of the Kingdom to the Samaritans and to the Gentiles, when He Himself said this was the will of the Father that sent Him? The only possible answer is that they were not yet ready to either understand or embrace and accept the full impact of His mission.

The Lord then admonished the twelve to open their eyes to the fields of harvest. Were their eyes already open, He would not admonish them to open them. Their eyes were not only closed to the Samaritans, they were completely blinded to them; blinded by a long history of bigotry toward them. Yet, the Lord saw a great harvest of souls among this ethnic group, and His desire was to see His disciples take part in that.

Following his short speech, the Lord again modeled His message in His life. Not only did He venture to go through Samaria. Not only did He initiate a discussion with a Samaritan woman. But against all Jewish behavior—the norms of His day—He stayed in Samaria for two days, whereby many from that town believed in Him (see John 4:39-42). The text does not explicitly state that the disciples were there with Jesus when He stayed at the Samaritan village, but the general assumption is that they were. Though it was a rather brief, two-day stay, this involved more than just a preaching activity on the part of Jesus and His disciples. This indicates that they talked, fellowshipped, ate, drank, and slept with those people. Jesus was modeling his disciple-making in very practical, down-to-earth ways.

Preaching at others, and even sharing our religious convictions without living them, usually does not have the same desired effects. At times, it can also create a negative backlash. If Jesus had contented Himself with simply speaking to those Samaritans as someone who owned the truth and them not, or if He had refused their invitation to stay with them, chances are they would have never believed in Him. This, regretfully, is what we set ourselves up against when we indicate in our Christian evangelism and traditional disciple-making methods that we are the sole owners of the truth. What is usually lacking is the practical modeling or actualization of our message in our lives, and this is exactly what the Lord did.

Jesus was so sympathetic to the Samaritans that the Jews accused Him of being a Samaritan and demon-possessed. John records that in chapter 8 of his gospel (John 8:47-49).

> He who belongs to God hears what God says. The reason you do not hear is that you do not belong to God. The Jews answered him, "Aren't we right in saying that you are a Samaritan and demon-possessed?" "I am not possessed by a demon," said Jesus, "but I honor my Father and you dishonor me."

It is worth noting in the text above that Jesus answered the second accusation in that He was not demon-possessed, but did not answer the first accusation in that He was a Samaritan, which leads the reader to believe that those two accusations were in reality only one, thus reflecting the Jewish attitude toward Samaritans in that they were impure and demon-possessed.

There are two other New Testament references where Jesus seems to be honoring Samaritans more than He did His own people. One is the famous parable of the Good Samaritan in Luke 10. The other is the testimony of the only leper of the ten Jesus healed who came back to give thanks, according to Luke 17. That leper was also a Samaritan (Luke 17:11-16).

So, whether in his teaching or, more important, modeled in His life, Jesus was seeking to influence His disciples to do away with their traditional and cultural baggage and begin to acquire Kingdom principles and values.

OF THE HOUSEHOLD OF ABRAHAM

Israel lived the generalized notion that since Abraham is the father of the nation, gaining favor with God was automatically granted. They did not have to earn it. They did not seem to realize that the promise of blessing Abraham's lineage was conditional. No sooner had John the Baptist launched his ministry than this issue surfaces. John did not hesitate to confront this arrogance in his call to repentance to those who came to his baptism (see Matthew 3:9). The same issue comes up in a heated debate between another group of Jews and Jesus (see John 8:39).

This generalized notion leaves us in little doubt in believing that the twelve inherited the same attitude and perspective.

So, how does Jesus deal with that in shaping his disciples?

In the Sermon on the Mount, according to Matthew chapters 5-7, the Lord pronounces a great number of new Kingdom principles. We have already looked at some aspects of that sermon in previous pages. What we will do here is to discuss further the methodology of the Lord in disciple-making. Much of this study will be based on what appeared in that sermon and how it was reflected in the life and actions of Jesus.

Against the backdrop of the generalized attitude of (being God-favored because of Abraham) the Jewish nation presented previously, and soon after Jesus completed His sermon, He entered Capernaum, his main city of dwelling, and was met by a Roman centurion, who asked him for help. Here is how Matthew 8:6-12 describes what followed:

> "Lord," he said, "my servant lies at home paralyzed and in terrible suffering." Jesus said to him, "I will go and heal him." The centurion replied, "Lord, I do not deserve to have you come under my roof. But just say the word, and my servant will be healed. For I myself am a man under authority, with soldiers under me. I tell this one, 'Go,' and he goes; and that one, 'Come,' and he comes. I say to my servant, 'Do this,' and he does it."

> When Jesus heard this, he was astonished and said to those following him, "I tell you the truth, I have not found anyone in Israel with such great faith. I say to you that many will come from the east and the west, and will take their places at the feast with Abraham, Isaac and Jacob in the kingdom of heaven. But the subjects of the kingdom will be thrown outside, into the darkness, where there will be weeping and gnashing of teeth." Then Jesus said to the centurion, "Go! It will be done just as you believed it would." And his servant was healed at that very hour.

There are a number of elements in this encounter that would have shocked any Jew of that day, including the disciples. First, there was the Roman Gentile centurion, a representative of the occupying power in Israel—therefore, an enemy—with unimpeded access to Jesus and to His healing powers.

Second, there was the incredible testimony of Jesus to the faith of this Roman soldier, whereby according to Him, such faith was not even found in Israel proper.

Third, Abraham is introduced in the story, except that the Jewish nation is not going to find automatic favor with God because of him. Rather, non-Jews will feast with him and with Isaac and Jacob in the Kingdom of heaven.

To the Jewish ears, these elements were scandalous, appalling, incriminatory, and chargeable. And further, Jesus goes on to say that "the subjects of the kingdom [meaning the Jewish nation], will be thrown outside" (Matthew 8:12).

Israel was the covenant nation through its father, Abraham. Was God turning His back on that covenant? Was God turning His back on Abraham? Was He forsaking His firstborn child, Israel? And for what? For going after the heathen, the dogs?

How else could Jesus begin to break the bonds that would chain the disciples to their erroneous and misguided covenantal understanding and expectations? These chains had thousands of years of history and had been passed from one generation to the next. The prophets of old had explained that the Abrahamic covenant was conditional. But that understanding did not make it into the public conscience.

By reaching out to an enemy, a gentile, and paving the way for him through his faith to become part of the household of Abraham, Jesus was introducing His new covenant, that which is not written on tablets of stone but in people's hearts. He was placing the first stones of a roadway that one day He would commission His disciples to take, as He sent them out to preach the good news of the Kingdom to the world.

Jesus would not allow ethnicity, race, color, or language come between Him and man He created in His image. The only thing that could come between Him and man was faithlessness. His mission was to teach and train His disciples similarly, modeling those teachings on His own life and example.

ROLE MODELING

The disciples had many other issues besides their traditional sense of God's favoritism toward their race. Mark, in the ninth chapter of his gospel, reveals to us a verbal quarrel that developed among the twelve while on their way to Capernaum. Here is the background to it, according to Mark 9:30-34:

They left that place and passed through Galilee. Jesus did not want anyone to know where they were, because he was teaching his disciples. He said to them, "The Son of Man is going to be betrayed into the hands of men. They will kill him, and after three days he will rise." But they did not understand what he meant and were afraid to ask him about it.

They came to Capernaum. When he was in the house, he asked them, "What were you arguing about on the road?" But they kept quiet because on the way they had argued about who was the greatest.

The context leads us to believe that once the disciples learned that Jesus was going to be killed, a strong loud argument ensued. Who was going to be in charge? Jesus did not present to them a clear line of succession. He did not appoint one or more to take over the leadership role, which is what the disciples humanly expected to see happen. They could not wait and, seemingly, they did not want to allow Jesus the time to work on that succession. They must have sensed that His departure was imminent and decided to take the matter into their own hands.

Not wanting to embarrass them, the Lord waited until they reached the house where they were staying and then asked them about what they were arguing so loudly. Not one of the twelve answered him, which leaves the reader to assume that they were all, without exception, involved in that dispute. Was it their pride that got in the way of disclosing to their Master what was going on, or was it their sense of shame? Mark does not answer that question. Yet, he does tell us about what they heatedly argued. They had been arguing about who was the greatest among them.

This is not the only time the Gospel writers disclosed that problem within the twelve. Matthew records for us in chapter 20 of his gospel another similarly embarrassing moment, initially involving two disciples and then developing into a dispute between those two and the remaining ten disciples (Matthew 20:17-21).

Now Jesus was going up to Jerusalem. On the way, he took the Twelve aside and said to them, "We are going up to Jerusalem, and the Son of Man will be delivered over to the chief priests and the teachers of the law. They will condemn him to death and will hand him over to the Gentiles to be mocked and flogged and crucified. On the third day he will be raised to life!" Then the mother of Zebedee's sons came to Jesus with her sons and, kneeling down, asked a favor of him. "What is it you want?" he asked. She said, "Grant that one of these two sons of mine may sit at your right and the other at your left in your kingdom."

For some reason, the publishers tend to make a break between verses 19 and 20, though they are interconnected. There is a direct correlation between the Lord foretelling his disciples of what was going to befall Him, in that He will be killed and raised again, and the mother of James and John, seeking special favors for her sons.

In the verses that followed, Matthew does not hide how he and the others took offense at that request, not so much because of the presumptuous attitude of the sons of Zebedee, rather that he and his nine other mates were left out of the equation. Here is his record of the quarrel that the request triggered (Matthew 20:24-28):

When the ten heard about this, they were indignant with the two brothers. Jesus called them together and said, "You know that the rulers of the Gentiles lord it over them, and their high officials exercise authority over them. Not so with you. Instead, whoever wants to become great among you must be your servant, and whoever wants to be first must be your slave—just as the Son of Man did not come to be served, but to serve, and to give his life as a ransom for many."

Such an attitude makes it hard for the coach to have a winning team on his side, even if that coach were Jesus. That may be one reason why when the Lord sent them on their first mission, He sent them in teams of twos, not all twelve together. He probably picked the easiest two who had a chance to make a small working team, knowing that if he were to send all twelve as one team, they would start bickering and would turn back halfway before getting there.

In short, Jesus did not have a team. He had twelve self-seeking and egoistic men grouped together. There was much work to try to make a team out of them. That was one challenge with which their Coach had to deal.

Teaching by Example

Did Jesus succeed? Yes, He did. But it took three plus years. How did He do it? What was His methodology? John gives us the answer in his gospel, chapter 13, verses 4-17. He writes:

> Jesus got up from the meal, took off his outer clothing, and wrapped a towel around his waist. After that, He poured water into a basin and began to wash his disciples' feet drying them with the towel that was wrapped around him. He came to Simon Peter, who said to him, "Lord, are you going to wash my feet?" Jesus replied, "You do not realize now what I am doing, but later you will understand." "No," said Peter, "you shall never wash my feet." Jesus answered, "Unless I wash you, you have no part with me." "Then, Lord," Simon Peter replied, "not just my feet but my hands and my head as well!" Jesus answered, "Those who have had a bath need only to wash their feet; their whole body is clean. And you are clean, though not every one of you." For he knew who was going to betray him, and that was why he said not every one was clean. When he had finished washing their feet, he put on his clothes and returned to his place. "Do you understand what I have done for you?" he asked them. "You call me 'Teacher' and 'Lord,' and rightly so, for that is what I am. Now that I, your Lord and Teacher, have washed your feet, you also should wash one another's feet. I have set you an example that you should do as I have done for you. Very truly I tell you, no servant is greater than his master, nor is a messenger greater than the one who sent him. Now that you know these things, you will be blessed if you do them.

The method that Jesus used cost Him much. It cost Him His self-esteem and his position. He was Master and Lord. Yet, in order for Him to use that method, he took on the position of a slave. This is exactly what slaves did. They washed the feet of their masters. Jesus could have chosen to use less costly methods. Why not just give them a handbook to read and have them answer the questions at the end? Yet, in His view, He felt that nothing surpassed teaching a lesson by personally living it out in front of one's learners.

It is obvious that most of us have taken the easy road when it comes to our Christian outreach and disciple-making. We have adopted the less costly method of doing the work. Less costly in time, less costly in effort, and more important, less costly in commitment! It may be that we did not know better. Or it may be that this is how we were trained ourselves, and we follow the pattern of those that preceded us. We did not very often see Christian teachers or pastors invite their learners to live with them and learn from their lives. That would be too much to ask. For some reason, it was not too much to ask for our Lord.

It is clear that the mission ahead was so important, grand, and inestimable that Jesus did not spare any effort in getting His message across, even if that cost Him His life, and it did. It is also clear that the messengers He was working with and working on were as dear as His own children, and more, He did not want them to fail. Their success would be His success, and their failure His failure. There was so much at stake.

What little time did the Lord have for Himself? How much privacy did He enjoy, except those times that He spent alone with His Father! Other than those times, every waking moment He spent with His twelve. That was the heart and soul of His disciple-making method.

As parents, we live all our lives before our children, and we do not have a problem with that. We patiently teach them how to walk and how to talk. We teach them how to read and how to write. We teach them how to play baseball and how to throw a basketball. We teach them their first prayer. We teach them just about everything there is to teach. Except, it is not by making them sit and take notes or by studying a booklet and doing homework. We do all the above and much more by living before them and with them. We walk. We talk. We read and write. We play and pray. And they follow suit and copy us. They make mistakes, but they learn. When they succeed, we, the parents, are exuberant. We succeed in their success.

In other words, it is not that the methodology of Jesus is so strange to us. We have used it with our own kids for ten, twenty, or possibly more years. Yet, most of us have miserably failed to see or to accept that very same methodology in regards to Christian outreach and disciple-making. It may be that we are not as committed to our learners as we are to our own children, and, therefore, are not willing to invest not only our time but our very lives in the process.

CHAPTER V

THE COST OF BECOMING A DISCIPLE
TO THE DISCIPLE

I magine Jesus inviting his disciples to bring their Bibles, their commentary books, their notebooks, and pens and sitting them down to take notes on living the Christian life. They all look up words in Hebrew and Aramaic for a word study. They look at verbs, structure, and context. They search the commentary books, looking for cultural and historical insights. They take turns asking questions and giving what insights they gleaned from the text. After an hour or two, they are sent home with homework. Their weekly meeting is over. Jesus or one of the followers closes in prayer. They agree to meet the following week and together check out what they did and how well they did it.

As they gather the following week, in the competitive spirit with which the human soul is endowed, each tries to outdo the other. They want good grades. There may not be actual degrees to be conferred; given the circumstances, a compliment from Jesus would do well enough. With Peter's habitual rush to speak, the others will do their best to keep him quiet. Their hot-tempered nature will drive James and John to find fault anyway, regardless of which other disciple speaks. The study they did has not changed them, despite their relative success at answering all the questions and getting passing grades. This is not to say that they did not also have a chance to also practice putting what they learned to the test. As a matter of fact, they presented their lesson materials to their friends and family members, who received them with very little enthusiasm.

We all know this is not how Jesus taught or trained His disciples. We know that He did not give them homework in the same way that we understand homework today. We also know there were no papers to correct, questions to answer, or commentary books to look at. We know all that and much more, because the invitation to becoming a disciple was fundamentally different from what most of us grew up with, read about, or with which we are familiar.

The call to discipleship that Jesus presented was a calling for all of one's life. Nothing short of that! Initially, life is a web of relationships: an infant's intimate relationship to his mother, a child's relationship to his father and siblings, followed by relating to mates at school and in the neighborhood. Soon, this young man meets a woman, and the two fall in love. They marry and start a new web of relationships, even more intimate than either one had experienced thus far. Add to this a person's relationships at the workplace and in the community at large, be it to his physician, dry cleaner, handyman, or mailman. Human relationships have a starting point but seem endless. The dots continue to add up day after day. Human relationships are not only part of life: they make human life possible. They are the threads that weave the very fabric of life.

Into all this came the challenging words of Jesus on what it meant to become a disciple: "'If anyone comes to Me and does not hate his father and mother, his wife and children, his brothers and sisters—yes, even his own life—he cannot be My disciple. And anyone who does not carry his cross and follow Me cannot be My disciple . . . In the same way, any of you who does not give up everything he has cannot be My disciple'" (Luke 14:26-27, 33).

These words are enough to make anybody cringe, and not only animal lovers, who are left wondering whether there was any room left for relating to one's pet dog, cat, or bird. The words of Jesus did not sound humanlike. They seemed to undo everything that man from the beginning of history considered sacred. Life potentially devoid of relationships becomes empty and meaningless. Forsaking one's possessions is one thing. Forsaking one's relationships is totally another.

But the Lord did not stop there. He took his words a measure or two beyond any human reason or logic. A disciple, according to Him, is also called to hate his own life. Hearing and reading these words, we begin to wonder how normative such disciples would be! How socially acceptable and accepting? How could a disciple ever get into a marriage relationship? And is not hate sinful to begin with? In what ways can a disciple be a loving person when he is to hate his own life?

As was the custom of rabbis, Jesus conveyed many of His messages in parables. Those were stories that rabbinical schools passed on from one generation of rabbis to another. Though Jesus repeated some of those same parables, there was one big exception: the endings were different. The door was not shut and locked in the face of the returning prodigal son. The man doing good to the victim on the road was not Jewish. It is not that the endings were meant to shock, yet they did.

Similarly with his teachings on becoming a disciple, other rabbis also had theirs. They had strict conditions and rules to follow. But none exacted the same price from his disciples as that demanded by Jesus from the one invited to follow Him. To the other rabbis, it was mostly following in their teachings. But not to Jesus! So, why so extreme? Why such language as hating oneself and potentially breaking every human relationship there is? Matthew records a similar challenge in his gospel, chapter 16 verse 25, where the Lord says to His hearers, "'Whoever wants to save his life will lose it, but whoever loses his life for me will find it.'"

Becoming a disciple of Christ is, in fact, costly. It may cost the disciple his or her family relationships, not that he or she will literally hate his or her parents, siblings, or immediate family. But by placing the love of God before any and all of these, he or she may alienate himself or herself from a more intimate relationship with them. More important though, a disciple should be willing to give up his own life, as many did in the early, turbulent centuries of the Christian faith, and as others continue to walk in their steps in hostile countries to this day. One's possessions, ambitions, ego, and ultimately, one's very life could be disposed of in the pursuit of becoming Christ's disciple.

Those words were not only hard to utter. They were harder to hear and heed. How much did the followers of Jesus understand? Did His words really sink in? And even if they did, were those words powerful enough to transform them into the disciples that the Lord meant them to be? The answer is no. The disciples themselves admit that as they recount how they all ran away when the Roman soldiers laid hands on Jesus in the Garden of Gethsemane. And before a maidservant and others, Peter had no qualms denying Jesus three times in a row. It becomes obvious that the disciples' own disciple-making process was not yet complete. They were still disciples in the making, and so they remained until the last day of their lives.

For three years, Jesus met on a very regular basis with his followers. He covered every aspect of the Christian life as they met. He did not tire giving them homework. He did not tire correcting their homework. He did not tire standing between them when they argued. And yet, at the end of those three years, nothing much had changed. The men of Galilee were the same. They were no more committed followers than on the first day they heard his invitation to forsake everything and follow Him. As it was, Peter, Andrew, James, and John went back to fishing at the first open occasion. They thought they had left that trade, and everyone else thought they did, too. But the trade was still entrenched in their hearts. With the Master now gone, there was nothing to stand between them and the Sea of Galilee. Maybe it was time for a second calling! A second touch!

In the end, the disciples did graduate. Their graduation ceremonies were different, but they were all painful and tragic. It is believed that Matthew gave his life in Ethiopia, after a sword was planted in his body. The Coptic Church of Egypt, also called St. Mark's Church, was given that name for the Gospel writer Mark, who was dragged by horses through the streets of Alexandria until he gave up his soul.

Luke was hanged in Greece; Peter was crucified upside down on an X-shaped cross. James, the son of Zebedee, was beheaded. James, the leader of the Jerusalem, church was initially thrown off a cliff and then beaten to death. With the exception of John, all the other disciples, including Paul, died a tragic martyr's death. Borrowing from Paul's second letter to Timothy, the disciples, like Paul, "fought the good fight, finished the race, [and] kept the faith" (2 Timothy 4:7).

The disciples had heard the call to discipleship. Yet, it is doubtful that they realized the full impact it would have on their lives and on the lives of their loved ones. They were enamored by the person of Christ. They were drawn to His teachings. They were awed by His power. But most of all, they were inspired by His example. He lived his own conditions for discipleship before any of them did. He carried his cross before they carried theirs. He was first to give up everything, including His very life. His requirements of discipleship were modeled in His life before, during, and after he placed those humanly unrealizable challenges before them. For if He were not willing to be the example Himself, what point was there in presenting those challenges in the first place, and what effects could He realistically expect to see in them?

While the emphasis in the previous pages seems to underline the cost of being a disciple to the disciple himself or herself, this only represents a brief introduction to something far more important in our study of Jesus as the Master discipler. Many good books have been written on Christian discipleship. A greater number of messages have been preached on that topic. In both cases, authors and preachers have largely based their exposition on the verses in the gospel of Luke. More often than not, the title that both author and speaker give to these verses is the same: the cost of discipleship. That is, the cost to the disciple.

Yet, in as much as authors and preachers wrote and spoke about the cost of discipleship to the disciple, they neglected to speak about the cost to the mentor, discipler, or disciple-maker. A churchgoing mentor, sitting in the pew and hearing such messages, or a mentor reading a book that discusses the cost of discipleship to the disciple, is left mostly untouched, unless, of course, he sees himself as a disciple also. Or unless he goes back to his own experience of when he was being discipled by somebody else. But as a disciple-maker or a mentor, he does not hear or recognize that there is any cost to him in carrying out his part of the process. Despite his involvement in the lives of his disciples, that involvement is at best marginal. He spends time on a weekly or bi-weekly basis, puts some effort into preparing for the next meeting, and hopefully takes time to pray for his disciples. But generally speaking, this is where his involvement ends. Yet, we all know that disciple-making the Jesus way was anything but that. The discussion in the following pages will take this up in greater detail.

CHAPTER VI

THE COST OF DISCIPLE-MAKING
TO THE DISCIPLE-MAKER

Jesus is given many titles in Scripture. Matthew introduced Him in the first chapter of his book as the Son of David, therefore, the legitimate heir to his throne (see Matthew 1:1). He then clarified and confirmed that with the testimony of the wise men before Herod, as they asked out loud, "'Where is He, King of the Jews?'" (see Matthew 2:2). After His baptism at the hands of John the Baptist, we come across and discover a qualitative and authoritative upgrade from being presented as the Son of David and King of the Jews to being referred to, not by Matthew and not by the wise men, but by heaven as "My beloved Son" (see Matthew 3:17). When the Tempter came to Him, that was the title He challenged in His words to Jesus, "'If you are the Son of God . . .'" (see Matthew 4:3).

Numerous books have been written about the Sonship of Jesus and His relationship to the Father. And while neither this book nor this chapter are meant to dig into deep theological issues, we still need to pause briefly at the mention of the term "son" as it relates to this study and, more specifically, to this chapter.

The term "son" denotes a unique set of relationships between two individuals. On the one side, namely the side of the son, such a relationship demands respect, obedience, and submission. On the other side, such a relationship dictates authority, power, and possibly control. These underlying thoughts permeate the New Testament, especially during those times when Jesus talked of His unique relationship to the Father. It is worth noting that in Matthew alone, Jesus used the word "Father" no less than forty times. A number of those uses describe God's fatherly attitude toward his creation. In others, Jesus added the possessive pronoun "your" before "Father" as He addressed the twelve. One example of that is found in Matthew 5:16, where Jesus exhorted His followers with the admonition, "'In the same way, let your light shine before men, that they may see your good deeds and praise your Father in heaven.'"

Of special interest to us are the references, both in Matthew as well as in the other Gospels, where Jesus specifically addressed God as His Father. The following is a sampling.

In Matthew 11:25, Jesus lifted up a song of homage to God: "At that time Jesus said, 'I praise you, Father, Lord of heaven and earth, because you have hidden these things from the wise and learned, and revealed them to little children.'"

Addressing the special favors James and John, the sons of Zebedee, were asking for, Jesus said to them, according to Matthew 20:23, "'You will indeed drink from my cup, but to sit at My right or left is not for Me to grant. These places belong to those for whom they have been prepared by my Father.'"

Answering the inquiry of the twelve regarding the timing of the events of the end times, of which He spoke in Matthew 23, Jesus offered an answer that has, over the ages, triggered even more questions. He said, according to Matthew 24:36, "'No one knows about that day or hour, not even the angels in heaven, nor the Son, but only the Father.'"

When faced with the prospect of the cross, Jesus lifted a prayer of supplication to His Father that the cup may be taken from Him. In His closing words, He said, "'Yet not as I will, but as you will'" (Matthew 26:42).

In other instances, Jesus referred to the temple as the "Father's house" and heaven as the "Father's Kingdom." To the Jews who sought to kill Him, according to John 5:18-19, Jesus made a shocking statement in that "The Son can do nothing of Himself."

In this short list, we discover quite a few revealing characteristics of the unique rapport between Jesus, as Son, and God the Father. These characteristics include offering praise, giving up control of the future, lifting up a supplication, yielding His will, and completely denying Himself the power to do anything of Himself.

Taken out of the larger context of the Gospels and emptied of the broader framework of the incarnation, such a list would send shivers to any believer and would raise one fundamental question: was Jesus truly a deity after all? The same references and others have given ammunition to a number of religions and schools of thought that continue to deny the divinity of Jesus.

So, what's in a title? As we just noted, everything could stand or potentially crumble with the proper understanding or misinterpretation of a title, in this case, the title "Son," as it refers to Jesus.

On the other hand, we have many more verses in the New Testament that unequivocally identify Jesus as God and, thus, attest to His claims of divinity. Here is a sampling.

John begins his gospel with the powerful testimony: "In the beginning was the Word, and the Word was with God, and the Word was God." He then goes on to clearly identify who the Word was in John 1:14: "And the Word became flesh."

Testifying to His eternal existence, Jesus said in John 8:58, "'Very truly I tell you,' Jesus answered, 'before Abraham was born, I am!'"

In His answer to Philip, according to John 14:9-10, Jesus leaves no doubt as to His true identity. He said: "'Don't you know me, Philip, even after I have been among you such a long time? Anyone who has seen me has seen the Father. How can you say, "Show us the Father"?'"

Silencing the Jews doubting his Messiahship, Jesus clearly stated in John 10:30, "'I and the Father are one.'"

To the Pharisees, who knew their Scriptures well and who sanctified the Sabbath as it was prescribed by Yahweh to Moses, Jesus said, according to Matthew 12:8, "'For the Son of Man is Lord of the Sabbath.'"

Assuring His disciples of His omnipresence, Jesus said in Matthew 18:20, "'For where two or three gather in my name, there am I with them.'"

Doubting Thomas fell on his knees before Jesus, exclaiming, "'My Lord and my God'" (John 20:28).

In his letter to the Colossians, Paul leaves no shadow of doubt as to the divine nature of Jesus. He wrote in his first chapter:

> The Son is the image of the invisible God, the firstborn over all creation. For in him all things were created: things in heaven and on earth, visible and invisible, whether thrones or powers or rulers or authorities; all things have been created through him and for him. He is before all things, and in him all things hold together. And he is the head of the body, the church; he is the beginning and the firstborn from among the dead, so that in everything he might have the supremacy. For God was pleased to have all his fullness dwell in him, and through him to reconcile to himself all things, whether things on earth or things in heaven, by making peace through his blood, shed on the cross.

Sorting through these two lists and other seemingly contradictory verses and references, we have an obligation as Bible students to accept one set and refute the other, refute both, or as Bible-believing Christians, look for the missing link between the two that would allow us to embrace both equally. That link is one simple term made up of three letters. This is the word "son."

While there are other innumerable references to the divinity of Jesus besides the ones quoted above, none present it as clearly or succinctly as Paul does in his letter to the church at Philippi, to whom He wrote: "Who, being in very nature God" (Philippians 2:6).

It can be argued that most if not all of the second list of references were used to testify to the divinity of our Lord. Yet, Paul's objective in that verse was not meant to prove the divinity of Jesus. It was, rather, an expression of the cost involved in the cross of Jesus. Paul expressed it by writing that Jesus, "did not consider equality with God something to be grasped, but made himself nothing, taking the very nature of a servant, being made in human likeness. And being found in appearance as a man, he humbled himself and became obedient to death—even death on a cross!" (Philippians 2:6-8)

It is one thing to be God and to be perceived as God, even if Deity took on a human form. It is very different to be God yet to be perceived as a slave. It is one thing to know Oneself to be God and to act as such. It is very different to know Oneself to be God and to act as if One is nothing! It is even one thing to be man, asking for such a simple thing as to have a life to live. It is another to forgo life in all its dimensions and offer one's life as the ultimate sacrifice. In Philippians 2:6-8, Jesus was not simply forgoing His rights and privileges as God; He was also forgoing them as man.

As Bible readers, Bible students, and even Bible scholars come across the miracles that Jesus performed, or read and contemplate insightful words of wisdom that He uttered, we and they pause to think whether Jesus was doing these in His Divine nature or in His human nature. Yet, the previously cited verses from the letter to the Philippians seem to indicate that Jesus shed His Divine powers, privileges, and rights and lived and acted as man. Otherwise, one could ask how and on what basis did He propose to his human disciples the ability to do more than He did, including moving mountains! For if He had engaged His divinity in the making of miracles, He could not possibly promise his human followers such divine powers! But if He performed those miracles and signs in His capacity as a human, empowered by the Spirit of God, the promise that they and we can do greater things by the same Spirit begins to sound reasonable and attainable.

We have two strikingly different actions and reactions that the Lord took that together seem to point to the same understanding previously described. One action and reaction is recorded for us in the gospel of John, chapter 11. Jesus stood before the cave where Lazarus was buried. He was moved to tears. Minutes later, He invoked the Father before calling out to the corpse to be raised. On the other hand, when faced with imminent danger in the Garden of Gethsemane, as hundreds of Roman soldiers surrounded Him and as He watched Peter take out his sword and strike the servant of the High Priest, Jesus denied Himself the authority to call on the Father to send heavenly troops to rescue Him.

In the first example, His humanity is clearly manifested in his tears and his invocation. In the second, His divinity is suppressed, shed aside, a clear actualization of what Paul spoke of in his letter to the Philippians. It is humanly impossible to begin to fathom the depths of sacrifice that Jesus as the Eternal Son of God endured in and through the incarnation process. It is only after His resurrection and the outpouring of the Holy Spirit that His disciples began to grasp the fullness of His true identity. Their repeated question as to His true Nature every time they witnessed one of His miracles was finally answered.

In His objective to make disciples, Jesus did not hesitate before any sacrifice or cringe before any challenge known to man. He, the Discipler, lived out in full submission to the Father as a Son and as a disciple. That was the example He set before His followers. And while He was One with the Father (see John 14), He made multiple references to the Father not because He was less Divine than the Father but because He was living out His humanity to the fullest.

A father figure in a modern Western context does not carry within it the rich, intricate, and unique relationships that tie such a figure to his offspring as it did in the Eastern mind-set, especially as it did in past generations. Not only was a son expected to be fully subordinate to his father, a son owed his very life to the father. References to one's father were always respectful. The father took on the first position in the family. He was the decision maker. He, in short, was the giver of life, and he had the authority to take it away.

John's gospel begins at the first verse with the eternality of the Word. In verse 14, John presents in four words what the greatest minds of our human race could never and can never comprehend: "The Word became flesh!"

We have in the Incarnation of the Word not only the greatest mystery of all times, but we also have the greatest act of self-deprecation and sacrifice. If man's arrogance and his desire to be like God is the most sinful attitude ever recorded, the Word taking on human flesh and blood is the most honorable act of grace and humbleness ever recorded. There is nothing that resembles it in human history, and there are no words in our dictionary that can grasp its eternal dimensions. God could not have fully shared in anything human unless He took on our humanity. The author of the letter to the Hebrews 4:15 wrote of Him as, "one who has been tempted in every way, just as we are." His identification with the human race was full and complete, with the exception of sin.

Peter and Andrew, and James and John, the sons of Zebedee, probably glorified in their skills as fishermen. Matthew may have been a successful tax collector. But whatever they or their colleagues had to give up to follow Jesus does not begin to compare with what He gave up to share in their and our humanity. There was not only a unique sense of humbleness. There was also a deeper sense of humility and humiliation. For the Creator of the universe to live in the flesh of a human body, with all its physical limitations, and undergo every aspect of bodily and physical maturity is unnerving and unsettling at best. Luke wrote in his gospel how, "Jesus grew in wisdom and stature, and in favor with God and men" (Luke 2:52). Was He ever reprimanded or spanked by His mother or by Joseph for something wrong He did not do? Did not His mother rebuke Him as a child when it was her and Joseph's mistake to begin their journey back home without checking to see where the child Jesus was (Luke 2:48)?

The very thought of God in the flesh being circumcised as an infant, thus allowing Him to become part of the people of God, is beyond our comprehension (see Luke 2:21). The very thought of God in the flesh identifying Himself with sinners and asking John the Baptist to immerse Him in the Jordan, as if He needed to fulfill that act of righteousness, is absolutely unheard of (see Matthew 3:13-17). To see God in the flesh tempted by Satan is extremely disconcerting (see Matthew 4:1-11). But the climax of it all was for the Son of God to become *sin* on our behalf and then die on a cross (see Corinthians 5:21 and Philippians 2:8). While by faith we accept that truth, the notion of a Holy God becoming sin and dying is utterly bizarre and humanly illogical. How the Giver of life could die is borderline foolish and insensible. And yet, it is in those same words that Paul described the wisdom of God to Greek philosophical thought (see 1 Corinthians 1:21-23).

The words of Jesus that "'No servant can be greater than his Master,'" according to John 15:20a, are not only true in those areas of greatness that we see in His Divine nature. They are not only true in His magnificent personality or overpowering love. But they also ring true in the area of cost and sacrifice, and that, in reality, is the very context in which those words were uttered. In the latter part of that same verse, John quotes the Lord saying, "'If they persecuted me, they will persecute you also.'" Jesus was greater in everything, including in His pain and suffering. The author of the letter to the Hebrews reminds all those that suffer to fix their eyes on, "Jesus, the author and perfecter of our faith, who for the joy set before him endured the cross, scorning its shame, and sat down at the right hand of the throne of God. Consider him who endured such opposition from sinful men, so that you will not grow weary and lose heart" (Hebrews 12:2-3).

In their Jewishness, the disciples had deep-seated issues with the Samaritans and with the Gentiles not because of what they did but because of who they were. Did Jesus not have issues with the sinners and tax collectors? He did, but not because of who they were, rather because of what they did. And yet, He set the example, making them his friends and eating and fellowshipping with them. How else would he be able to influence them? Was He not scorned by His own people for doing that?

Did Jesus not feel the same humiliation His Jewish people felt under the Roman occupation? Did he not nickname Herod a "fox" (Luke 13:32)? Was not the temptation to rule the kingdoms of the earth that Satan offered to Him real, and was it not replicated in the crowds wanting to kidnap and make Him king of an independent nation? Was not the temptation for expediency in turning stone into bread appealing? Did he not experience betrayal by a trusted friend? Did He not sense the need to be in fellowship with the Father in prayer? Did He not hunger and thirst? Was He never tempted to sleep rather than spend the night in prayer? Was He not persecuted and killed despite His innocence?

All those questions, and many more, have the same answer, and it is yes. Briefly stated, there was no human feeling in the physical, emotional, or spiritual sense that Jesus did not live through, except a sense of guilt and shame that results from committing sin. That He did not know, because there was no sin in Him.

The very Son of God, by His incarnation, became the son of man, born to a poor carpenter. It was in those same terms that he was identified by his countrymen (Matthew 13:55). That perspective may shed a light on why the Pharisees or the scribes or the more learned strata of the Jewish society of His day would not even consider following Him. In part, that explains his personal choice of disciples, inviting nobodies—in the likes of fishermen and tax collectors—to follow him. His entourage provided an excellent commentary of what He chose to be his parental background. Unlike us, He could have chosen to be born, as the wise men of the East expected, in a king's palace. But He chose not to be. His humbleness was evident from the day the news was announced to a poor virgin from Galilee. Every aspect of His life, beginning with his refugee status in Egypt and everything that followed, only proved his totally human orientation. At a time when human kings saw themselves as semi-gods, the God and King of heaven and earth made Himself a human slave before His Father.

Jesus could have battled the Evil One using His Divine powers. Yet, in His full humanity, He chose to battle Him with the Word, thus setting an example before us humans. When presented with the tempting invitation of the crowds to be acclaimed as king, He withdrew and spent the time in prayer. If anything, that was a clue to His natural human urge to submit to such a dazzling seduction and to using human means to resist it.

At the expense of being completely misunderstood, of being falsely accused of lack of concern for a family member, and more important, of being discredited as a man of miracles, Jesus does not succumb to the human pressure of seeing John freed from his prison cell and from sure death. The Gospels do not give too many details, yet if Jesus shed tears before the tomb of Lazarus, He surely shed as many tears at John's departure.

The list of the manifestations of the humble humanity of Jesus as the Son of Man is endless, He who had no place to call home. He who felt the need to spend sleepless nights in prayer and days on end in fasting. He, the Holy One, was accused of breaking the Sabbath, of blasphemy, of not being religious or holy enough for the religious establishment of His day. At some point in His ministry, He earned the very derisive title of Samaritan and at some point, was being called the "devil in the flesh" (Matthew 10:25). He was not even spared ridicule over His eating and drinking habits, and thus scorned as a glutton and a drunkard.

His compatriots may have questioned His divinity, but they never questioned His humanity. To them, He was one of their own, to the point of looking at Him with disdain. The divine secret of the Son of God coming in the flesh was not revealed to them. Jesus had lived out His humanity to the fullest. Or as Paul said, "Who, being in very nature God, did not consider equality with God something to be used to his own advantage; rather, he made himself nothing by taking the very nature of a servant, being made in human likeness" (Philippians 2:6-7). Jesus did not succumb to the pressure of proving His Deity, He Who was the Son of God and, in time, became the Son of Man! Our minds will never comprehend the cost for Him to take on human flesh.

Some Old Testament and New Testament publications tend to summarize what is believed to be the central thought in a chapter or in a paragraph and then place that short title on top. One of those paragraphs appears in the gospel of Matthew (Matthew 8:18-22). The publisher felt that the title "The Cost of Following Jesus" captured the essence of those verses. Here is what those verses state:

> When Jesus saw the crowd around him, he gave orders to cross to the other side of the lake. Then a teacher of the law came to him and said, "Teacher, I will follow you wherever you go." Jesus replied, "Foxes have holes and birds of the air have nests, but the Son of Man has no place to lay his head." Another disciple said to him, "Lord, first let me go and bury my father." But Jesus told him, "Follow me, and let the dead bury their own dead."

While it may be partly befitting to choose "The Cost of Following Jesus" as a title for the verses above, there is another side to those same verses that is not reflected in this title, especially as we look at verse 20. It is true that Jesus was laying the cost of following Him before the teacher of the Law and before another disciple. Yet, He was not asking something that He was not willing to pay Himself. His demands for commitment and sacrifice are only echoes of His personal commitment and sacrifice. There is as much cost to the master as there is to the disciple, and often more, and as in the case above, the master always bears the cost first. Otherwise, the example is missing.

The call to disciple is a very demanding enterprise, more so to the discipler than to the disciple. Could it be that many of us have failed to see more committed disciples because we had failed to set the example of commitment before them?

CHAPTER VII

THE VALUE OF SUFFERING IN DISCIPLE-MAKING

We discussed in the previous chapter the cost of disciple-making to both the discipler and to the disciple-to-be. In this chapter, the discussion will be limited to whether and in what ways Christ approached suffering as a tool in his disciple-making strategy and process. It is worth noting that this chapter does not deal with the issue of suffering in its entire scope. That is not the intention here, though there will be clues that may help one better understand some aspects of the dilemma of suffering in the world.

The Bible text in Genesis leaves no doubt to its reader that pain and suffering entered the world as a direct and unavoidable result of sin (see Genesis 2:17). Following that are multiple warnings from God of dire consequences for the house of Israel and for the nations of the world if they did not abide by His laws (see Isaiah chapters 13-23). And then, throughout the pages of the Jewish Bible, one reads firsthand whole chapters filled with descriptions of the actual judgment that befell the Jewish nation and other nations as a result of turning away from the Lord. God acted on His warnings. Sin was punishable by every type of pain.

That principle of cause and effect between sin and suffering became well established in the national conscience as well as in the mind and heart of every Jewish believer. It was this view that the disciples of Jesus had come to adopt, in sync with what their recorded sacred writings described and what their revered rabbis taught.

It is, therefore, no surprise that at the sight of a man born blind, the disciples immediately made the connection between sin and suffering and went to their Master, according to John 9:2, asking, "Rabbi, who sinned, this man or his parents, that he was born blind?" Their minds were set, and their assumptions were rock solid. Someone must have sinned. The disciples passed their verdict without any room for appeal. Either the blind man or his parents were guilty. His blindness was enough proof. They only needed to know the culprit.

Yet, there was a big disconnect, an absence of sheer common sense in the disciples' accusation. On what basis did they ask if it was this man's personal sin that led to his blindness when he was born like that? In what sense did he commit sin before his own birth?

The teachers of the Law, the Pharisees, held exactly the same position vis-à-vis this blind man. In their questioning, they, too, passed judgment against him and his parents, thus representing the same school of thought. According to John 9:34, they said to him, "'You were steeped in sin at birth; how dare you lecture us!'"

A few cases are recorded for us in the Gospels. One of those is in Matthew 9, where the Lord Himself brings up the direct correlation between sin and sickness. This is the case of the paralyzed man who was brought on a mat before Jesus. Addressing this man, Jesus said, "'Take heart, son; your sins are forgiven'" (Matthew 9:2b).

In John 5, we see the Lord visit the pool of Bethesda, where he grants healing to an invalid. Jesus later finds the man at the temple and warns him, saying, "'See, you are well again. Stop sinning or something worse may happen to you'" (John 5:14).

In other instances, no explicit mention is made to denote a connection between sin and sickness. One such case is found in Matthew 9:27-31:

> As Jesus went on from there, two blind men followed him, calling out, "Have mercy on us, Son of David!" When he had gone indoors, the blind men came to him, and he asked them, "Do you believe that I am able to do this?" "Yes, Lord," they replied. Then he

touched their eyes and said, "According to your faith let it be done to you"; and their sight was restored.

Contrasted with the above references, John 9:2 stands out in the Gospels as the only time where the Lord is quoted to have confronted a misplaced judgmental attitude and where He began to address the seemingly unquestionable correlation between sin and suffering. His response surely took the disciples by surprise, when He answered them, "'Neither this man nor his parents sinned.'"

By making this statement, Jesus was creating a huge paradigm shift for His disciples and contemporaries. The obvious was not always true. Jumping to conclusions based on outward appearance can be unfortunate and very misleading. Seeking to have an answer to the "why" can spiritually blind the person from understanding the "what for."

Jesus then went on to add, "'This happened so that the works of God might be displayed in him'" (John 9:3). Jesus thus elevated man's suffering to an altogether new level. According to Him, man's suffering can potentially be used for a higher, divine purpose. It can have a direct impact on heaven itself. Suffering—even as devastating to the parents as having a child born blind or as disastrous as denying the affected individual any real hope in the world of seers—can have a tremendously positive value from a heavenly perspective.

John chapter 11 sheds very important light on another widely misunderstood aspect of human suffering as it relates to a loving God. Lazarus, the only brother to Mary and Martha, was sick and nearing death. In their message to the Master, imploring Him to come immediately, Mary and Martha sent a very unique message. "'Lord,' the word said, "'the one you love is sick'" (John 11:3).

How do we put these two elements together: Godly love and human sickness? If God loved the world, would He not keep it safe from all harm? Herein comes the faith of a deist, who, while believing that there is a God, thinks God is absent from the world stage, uninterested in human affairs, and definitely indifferent to human pain and suffering.

Or on a more personal level, why would Jesus treat the friend he loved, Lazarus, the way He did? The two sisters for sure expected differently. And they based their expectations on the fact that Jesus loved him. Yet, rather than rushing to his bedside, Jesus tarried two more days. Nonetheless, He made a very important comment. He said, "'It is for God's glory.'"

Here again, similar to his comment when the disciples asked him if it was the man born blind or his parents who sinned, Jesus brought into the discussion a new element, often overlooked when it comes to human suffering. This is the fact that God would use suffering for a noble purpose: that such suffering could have a positive influence on earth, as well as on heaven itself. In the case of Lazarus, the Person of God Himself was going to be glorified.

One more time, Jesus tried to break the template that the nation had developed over the centuries and to which the disciples conformed. He was trying to show through his encounter with the man born blind and then in the sickness of his friend Lazarus that pain and suffering can be purposeful, and they need not be the result of sin. Additionally, as in the case of Lazarus, we are not to doubt the love of God toward us just because He allows us to get sick or because He may tarry in providing healing, or He may deny it altogether!

We do not know how and to what extent the hardships recorded in the Hebrew Bible about such prophets as Job or Jeremiah impacted the disciples. It is only fair to assume that the notion of someone being righteous and still being inflicted with pain was not totally strange to them.

What we do know for certain is that at the very start of His earthly ministry, Jesus brought this concept to the forefront. In His first recorded discourse in Matthew 5, and in the first few verses, which outline general principles that govern the Kingdom of heaven, Jesus gave the following warning: "'Blessed are those who are persecuted because of righteousness, for theirs is the kingdom of heaven'" (Matthew 5:10).

It is quite interesting to note the change in pronouns in the verses that follow, meaning verses 11 and 12. The warning in verse 10 was generalized. Jesus did not address the disciples or the crowd specifically, though obviously they could hear Him. He only identified the persecuted as "those" who live righteously. But in the next two verses, He deliberately addressed the disciples. He said, "'Blessed are you when people insult you, persecute you and falsely say all kinds of evil against you because of me. Rejoice and be glad, because great is your reward in heaven, for in the same way they persecuted the prophets who were before you'" (Matthew 5:11-12).

Referring to "those" in verse 10, it is quite probable that the disciples did not even pay much attention. "Those" could mean anybody, not necessarily them. The next phrase, though, did catch all their attention. Jesus was upping the ante with his words, "'Blessed are you when people insult you.'" This was no more a question of the odds of whether the disciples were going to be persecuted. The words of Jesus were as prophetic as any other prophetic statement he would make. To make sure His words were well understood, Jesus then reminds them of the prophets of old, who were also persecuted. We note that in these two verses, meaning Matthew 5:11-12, Jesus used the pronouns "you" and "your" five times, as He referred to the disciples.

Despite the clarity of the words of Jesus, it is doubtful that the disciples thought much of these warnings at the time. If anything, they could relegate the persecution that Jesus seemed to speak of to the distant unknown future.

Lest the disciples forget the one-verse warning of Matthew 5:11, Jesus, according to Matthew 10:16-42, gave a whole discourse, listing all types of suffering that the disciples were most certainly going to face as they were sent on their first mission. Here is how Matthew records that discourse.

> "I am sending you out like sheep among wolves. Therefore be as shrewd as snakes and as innocent as doves. Be on your guard; you will be handed over to the local councils and be flogged in the synagogues. On my account you will be brought before governors

and kings as witnesses to them and to the Gentiles. But when they arrest you, do not worry about what to say or how to say it. At that time you will be given what to say, for it will not be you speaking, but the Spirit of your Father speaking through you.

"Brother will betray brother to death, and a father his child; children will rebel against their parents and have them put to death. You will be hated by everyone because of me, but the one who stands firm to the end will be saved. When you are persecuted in one place, flee to another. Truly I tell you, you will not finish going through the towns of Israel before the Son of Man comes.

"The student is not above the teacher, nor a servant above his master. It is enough for students to be like their teachers, and servants like their masters. If the head of the house has been called Beelzebul, how much more the members of his household!

"So do not be afraid of them, for there is nothing concealed that will not be disclosed, or hidden that will not be made known. What I tell you in the dark, speak in the daylight; what is whispered in your ear, proclaim from the roofs. Do not be afraid of those who kill the body but cannot kill the soul. Rather, be afraid of the One who can destroy both soul and body in hell. Are not two sparrows sold for a penny? Yet not one of them will fall to the ground outside your Father's care. And even the very hairs of your head are all numbered. So don't be afraid; you are worth more than many sparrows.

"Whoever acknowledges me before others, I will also acknowledge before my Father in heaven. But whoever disowns me before others, I will disown before my Father in heaven.

"Do not suppose that I have come to bring peace to the earth. I did not come to bring peace, but a sword. For I have come to turn a man against his father, a daughter against her mother, a daughter-in-law against her mother-in-law—a man's enemies will be the members of his own household.

"Anyone who loves their father or mother more than me is not worthy of me; anyone who loves their son or daughter more than me is not worthy of me. Whoever does not take up their cross and follow me is not worthy of me. Whoever finds their life will lose it, and whoever loses their life for my sake will find it.

"Anyone who welcomes you welcomes me, and anyone who welcomes me welcomes the one who sent me. Whoever welcomes a prophet as a prophet will receive a prophet's reward, and whoever welcomes a righteous person as a righteous person will receive a righteous person's reward. And if anyone gives even a cup of cold water to one of these little ones who is my disciple, truly I tell you, that person will certainly not lose their reward."

The one common denominator between what Jesus said in all four contexts referenced above is that we cannot content ourselves by looking at suffering from a human standpoint. In other words, there is a higher divine purpose, a divine heavenly dimension that, if understood properly, would completely redefine suffering.

As we continue to make our way in the gospel of Matthew, we are confronted with a perplexing discovery in Matthew 16. Here is how Matthew records the incident between the Lord and Peter in verses 21 to 27:

From that time on Jesus began to explain to his disciples that he must go to Jerusalem and suffer many things at the hands of the elders, the chief priests and the teachers of the law, and that he must be killed and on the third day be raised to life.

Peter took him aside and began to rebuke him. "Never, Lord!" he said. "This shall never happen to you!"

Jesus turned and said to Peter, "Get behind me, Satan! You are a stumbling block to me; you do not have in mind the concerns of God, but merely human concerns."

Then Jesus said to his disciples, "Whoever wants to be my disciple must deny themselves and take up their cross and follow me. For whoever wants to save their life will lose it, but whoever loses their life for me will find it. What good will it be for someone to gain the whole world, yet forfeit their soul? Or what can anyone give in exchange for their soul? For the Son of Man is going to come in his Father's glory with his angels, and then he will reward each person according to what they have done.

Peter loved Jesus and obviously did not wish him any harm. On the other hand, we know that the disciples, including Peter, expected Jesus to be the next revolutionary, working His way to an independent state. Those two elements could potentially explain Peter's strong reaction to the revelation Jesus made.

Yet, as we look more closely at what Jesus said, we note that it was not the Romans who were going to kill Him. Thus, He was not referring to an insurrection that He would lead against the occupiers, which could possibly lead to a sentence of death. Rather, He indicated that it would be the religious Jewish establishment that would be after Him and have Him killed. So, did Peter react simply out of love for His Master, or was he reacting against the religious establishment, or both? Or could it be that Peter feared for his own life if His master were to be killed? Was this what Jesus meant when He said to him that he had, "'merely human concerns'"?

One thing is certain though. Peter did not listen well. He did not hear Jesus speak of His resurrection. All he heard was of the sufferings that Jesus would face and of his death.

The language that Jesus used to rebuke Peter is even stronger than Peter's reaction. To Jesus, Peter was a mouthpiece of Satan. This is the only time in the Gospels where Jesus addressed anybody using such strong language. Even when He sent word to Herod, he said to go tell that "fox."

So, why did Jesus use such strong language to a disciple who loved Him, defended Him, and even offered to die with Him (see Matthew 26:35). When the soldiers and Jewish officials came to the Garden of

Gethsemane to arrest Jesus, Peter did not hesitate to use his sword in His defense (see John 18:10).

In his spiritual shortsightedness, Peter failed to understand the need for redemption. Despite his Jewish upbringing, he failed to see such important Messianic portions of the Hebrew Bible as Isaiah 53 or Psalm 22, or other Suffering Servant songs that describe in detail all that the Messiah was going to go through. Whether it was his love toward His Master or his fear of a future without Him, Peter could not grasp the need for suffering as a means of redemption. Jesus had not failed to clearly state that He "must" go to Jerusalem. This was not to be questioned. There was no life without the cross. There could not be salvation without dying.

Peter knew well his personal need for a savior. In his boat, according to Luke 5:8, Peter fell on his knees before Jesus and admitted his sinfulness. He said, "'Go away from me, Lord; I am a sinful man!'" In other words, Peter saw his need for a Messiah to save him from sin. But what he miserably failed to see, and even tried to stop, was allowing the Messiah to suffer. His words expressed complete disallowance and unmitigated rejection of the prospect of seeing the Messiah suffer and die.

What is said of Peter—and more—can be said of his mates. Take the example of the two disciples walking back to Emmaus, who after the Lord had died and risen again, were still questioning the dramatic experiences they had witnessed and their impact on their lives. They, too, could not comprehend why, "the one who was going to redeem Israel," was sentenced to death and was crucified (Luke 24:18-24). It seems from this text that their understanding of "redemption" had only social and political implications. It was only after the outpouring of the Holy Spirit on Pentecost that the apostles finally grasped the full picture. This is when they finally understood what true redemption was and the ultimate sacrifice that was needed to accomplish it.

As in previous chapters, where we discussed the methodology that Jesus used to mold His disciples-to-be, so it was with the final act of redemption. He set the example by suffering and dying Himself.

It is in the light of this act of redemption that the author of the letter to the Hebrews wrote the following: "Therefore, since we are surrounded by such a great cloud of witnesses, let us throw off everything that hinders and the sin that so easily entangles. And let us run with perseverance the race marked out for us, fixing our eyes on Jesus, the pioneer and perfecter of faith. For the joy set before him he endured the cross, scorning its shame, and sat down at the right hand of the throne of God. Consider him who endured such opposition from sinners, so that you will not grow weary and lose heart. In your struggle against sin, you have not yet resisted to the point of shedding your blood" (Hebrews 12:1-4).

It is also in the light of the same that Paul wrote in his letter to the Philippians, "I want to know Christ—yes, to know the power of his resurrection and participation in his sufferings, becoming like him in his death, and so, somehow, attaining to the resurrection from the dead" (Philippians 3:10-11).

We see the same in the lives of all the apostles, as recorded in Acts 5:41: "The apostles left the Sanhedrin, rejoicing because they had been counted worthy of suffering disgrace for the Name."

Christ had succeeded. Not only had His prophetic pronouncements of persecution—as they appeared in Matthew 5, 10, and elsewhere—been fully realized, they were realized with joy. The reason? The disciples, now turned apostles carrying His message, finally understood the purpose for which God can and does use suffering, especially in the life of a believer: namely, for its redemptive value in his own life, as well as in the lives of others!

Teaching someone to accept or to appreciate suffering for one's faith is a very challenging responsibility. Jesus knew that and experienced it firsthand with his disciples. This is why He did what He does best: set the example. The cross was a must not only as a means of redeeming a fallen world. It was also a cross He carried before them so that each and every follower can carry his cross in the same manner. A disciple carries his cross so that in the end, like the Master, he can be carried on it! A disciple carries his cross so that in the end, like the Master, his cross will have a redemptive value in the lives of others.

What types of redemptive values can someone glean from one's own suffering or from the suffering of another? Chief among these would be knowing Christ. We think of Saul of Tarsus and the apostle Paul, and how he was struck on his way to Damascus before putting his faith in Christ. We also think of him in his sufferings, which were used by God to lead many Jews and gentiles to Himself. A Christian can learn to have more faith, patience, joy, or others of the fruit of the Spirit both through his own sufferings and those of others. These also qualify to be called redemptive values.

In First Peter 4:1-2, the apostle wrote the following: "Therefore, since Christ suffered in his body, arm yourselves also with the same attitude, because whoever suffers in the body is done with sin. As a result, they do not live the rest of their earthly lives for evil human desires, but rather for the will of God."

In short, the list of redemptive values that can be reaped through suffering is endless. The lesson to be learned for us is the following: rather than ask the question "why" every time the Lord allows us or others to suffer, maybe we should ask the question, "what redemptive value is God trying to grow in us or in others through us?" And while the Lord may be using suffering to lead us to repentance from sin, it also qualifies as redemptive value.

In closing this chapter, I would like to underline one last point. According to the text from Hebrews 12, quoted previously, we can begin to understand the unfathomable redemptive value that Christ wrought through His suffering and death, whereby Jesus could do what He did, "for the joy set before him." From heaven's perspective, it was worth it all. So much was hanging on the sufferings and death of Christ. So much can also be hanging on our suffering as Christians, if only we allow God to use it to His glory and to carry a redemptive value in our own lives and in the lives of others.

CHAPTER VIII

SETTING THE EXAMPLE IN FORGIVENESS

The message was the same, but the reaction was quite different. I am here making reference to one event and one encounter in the life of Jesus. The event is that of calming the storm on the Sea of Galilee, as we read it in the gospels of Matthew, Mark, and Luke. The encounter is with the paralyzed man whose sins were forgiven.

Here is Matthew's rendering of the calming of the Sea of Galilee, as he records it in chapter 8:23-26:

> Then he got into the boat and his disciples followed him. Suddenly a furious storm came up on the lake, so that the waves swept over the boat. But Jesus was sleeping. The disciples went and woke him, saying, "Lord, save us! We're going to drown!" He replied, "You of little faith, why are you so afraid?" Then he got up and rebuked the winds and the waves, and it was completely calm.

On witnessing this dramatic event, the disciple's reaction was one of amazement and wonder. Matthew invites us to listen to them as they exclaim, "What kind of man is this? Even the winds and the waves obey him!" We do not know if those words were followed by a theological debate among the twelve on the true identity of the Lord.

89

On the other hand, when, according to Matthew 9:2, a paralyzed man lying on a mat is brought to Jesus, and Jesus says to him, "'Take heart, son; your sins are forgiven,'" Matthew is completely silent as to any reaction from the twelve. There is no awe or amazement. The ones who show a strong negative reaction are the teachers of the Law, who said, "'This fellow is blaspheming!'" (Matthew 9:3).

So, how come the disciples were filled with wonder at the calming of the sea but seemingly did not utter a word at the forgiving of this man's sins? Is it because they could see the effects of His words in the first case, while the effect of his words to the paralyzed man was something that the man alone could experience internally? Or is it because they did not fully comprehend the breadth and depth of the statement he made to the paralyzed man? Or maybe some shared the view that the teachers of the Law had but were too timid to express that!

Whatever the reason, though, it is quite interesting to look at the reaction of the teachers of the Law, who obviously saw the theological reach of the words of Jesus. To them, Jesus had blasphemed. He had made Himself equal to God by attributing to Himself God's unique authority to forgive sins. "'Who can forgive sins but God alone?'" the teachers ask according to Mark 2:7.

To both groups, the twelve and the teachers of the Law, Jesus was a mere man. Matthew records for us the reaction of the crowds, who he says, "were filled with awe; and they praised God, who had given such authority to man" (Matthew 9:8).

The crowds did not understand that Jesus is equal to God and could, therefore, grant forgiveness on His behalf. Neither did the twelve nor the teachers of the Law. As important, none of those three groups could grasp or assimilate that when Jesus forgave the man His sins, He was forgiving him his sins against Himself. For as valid as it may be for Jesus, being God's equal, to forgive on behalf of God, that does not compare to the fact that Jesus could do that fully, because that man had sinned against His Person. In that sense, Jesus had every right to withhold forgiveness or to grant it. In other words, Jesus was not forgiving sins committed against "someone" else. That is always easy to do, regardless of whether such forgiveness is valid. Jesus was forgiving the man his sins against Him, being One with the Father.

The paralyzed man in Matthew 9 was not the only individual who was pardoned for his sin. The sinful woman at Simon the Pharisee's house was also granted forgiveness. We read that in Luke 7:48, where Jesus freely offered her forgiveness for her sins with the words, "'Your sins are forgiven.'"

In John 8, we read how the teachers of the Law and the Pharisees brought before Jesus a woman caught in adultery. In verse 11 of that chapter, the Lord sent her away, with an admonition to leave her life of sin. But He stopped short of condemning her.

There are other texts in the New Testament, where the Lord Jesus clearly stated to the twelve that He was authorized to speak on behalf of heaven itself when it comes to the forgiving of sins. We see that in the context of the prayer that He taught His disciples in Matthew 6. At the close of that prayer, Jesus made a promise and sounded a warning. The promise he made is encapsulated in the words, "'For if you forgive other people when they sin against you, your heavenly Father will also forgive you.'" Following that, He immediately added the warning, "'But if you do not forgive others their sins, your Father will not forgive your sins'" (Matthew 6:14-15). These verses make it crystal clear that Jesus could authoritatively speak for the Father.

To help further clarify the above, we take the example of Peter in his encounter with Simon, the man who practiced sorcery and who, according to the book of Acts 8, sought to purchase the gift of the Spirit. Responding to his sinful and selfish request, Peter could only say to him, "Repent of this wickedness and pray to the Lord in the hope that he may forgive you for having such a thought in your heart. For I see that you are full of bitterness and captive to sin" (Acts 8:22-23). Peter was not in a position to forgive this man's sins or promise that God would surely do that for him. Jesus, as we saw previously, could do both without hesitation.

As discussed in earlier chapters of this book, every time Jesus performed a miracle, presented truths about the Kingdom of God, or anything in between—including but not limited to granting forgiveness, as we read previously—He did as His means of shaping the twelve to carry His message after Him. When Peter came to Him, according to Matthew 18:21, he asked, "'Lord, how many times shall I forgive my brother or sister who sins against me? Up to seven times?'" The Lord placed before him what sounds like a human impossibility. He said to him, "'Not seven times, but seventy-seven times.'" Some commentators have said this means seven to the power seventy, rather than the 490 times that the reader generally assumes is meant.

But as with other Kingdom principles, the Lord did not stop at simply teaching by word of mouth. His was more the incarnational rather than the propositional model of imparting truth and molding the twelve. So, as he imparted forgiveness to the paralyzed man, and as He granted forgiveness to the sinful woman at Simon's house, and as he declined from pronouncing judgment against the woman who was caught in sin, the time came for Him to personalize all that. Though, as explained above, Jesus did forgive, because being One with God, every trespass against God was trespass against Him. Yet, such may not be the perception of those witnessing such acts of forgiveness. So, in order to personalize that in indelible ways before the twelve and before the watching world, Jesus exercised what he preached as He hung on the cross at Golgotha. There, according to Luke 23:34, Jesus said, "'Father, forgive them, for they do not know what they are doing.'"

The twelve had witnessed every aspect of insult, physical and emotional abuse, humiliation, and disgrace that their Lord had suffered at the hands of the religious, Jewish establishment and at the hands of the Roman occupier. At the fullness of it all, their Master and their Lord pleaded for forgiveness rather than revenge. He pleaded for mercy rather than judgment. He prayed for clemency rather than vindictiveness. In the Garden of Gethsemane, as Peter drew his sword and struck the servant of the high priest, Jesus turned to him and said, "'Do you think I cannot call on my Father, and he will at once put at my disposal more than twelve legions of angels?'" (Matthew 26:53).

But that was not to be. Not only did Jesus not retaliate, he went the second mile and granted forgiveness to those who crucified Him.

What could possibly take away the vengeful attitude of James and John toward the Samaritans? Outside the outpouring of the Holy Spirit on the day of Pentecost and the living example that the Lord modeled nothing, would have.

Was it not with the Spirit and attitude of the Master that the author of the letter to the Hebrews penned the words in 12:4, "Consider him who endured such opposition from sinners, so that you will not grow weary and lose heart."

Paul set the standard for forgiveness when he wrote to the Christian community at Colossi, "Bear with each other and forgive one another if any of you has a grievance against someone. Forgive as the Lord forgave you" (Colossians 3:13). In his letter to the Ephesians 4:32, he again admonished them to, "Be kind and compassionate to one another, forgiving each other, just as in Christ God forgave you." That standard was the forgiveness that Christ granted them.

Peter, the disciple who seemingly had personal issues with forgiveness, wrote in his first epistle, 2:18-21, "Slaves, in reverent fear of God submit yourselves to your masters, not only to those who are good and considerate, but also to those who are harsh. For it is commendable if someone bears up under the pain of unjust suffering because they are conscious of God. But how is it to your credit if you receive a beating for doing wrong and endure it? But if you suffer for doing good and you endure it, this is commendable before God. To this you were called, because Christ suffered for you, leaving you an example, that you should follow in his steps."

It is hardly conceivable that anyone could be called Christian if that person did not demonstrate the same spirit of forgiveness that the Master so lived. That, as much or more than any other quality, is the sign of a true disciple.

CHAPTER IX

THE LORD OF SECOND CHANCES

Before the tomb of Lazarus, Jesus called only once for him to come out and Lazarus did (John 11:43). Approaching the town of Nain, Jesus encountered a funeral procession of a widow's only son. Addressing the dead man, Jesus said, "'Young man, I say to you, get up!'" He said that once, and the dead man sat up and began to talk (Luke 7:14-15). Standing in a boat on the stormy Sea of Galilee, Jesus had only to rebuke and command it one time, saying, "'Quiet! Be still!'" The wind died down, and it was completely calm (Mark 4:39).

The question that can haunt a Bible reader, and potentially also a Bible student, is the exception to this general observation, as we read of that in the gospel of Mark 8, with special emphasis on verse 25, where the Lord put His hands on the man's eyes two times before his sight was fully restored. Here is how Mark presents the details surrounding this event in verses 22 to 26:

> They came to Bethsaida, and some people brought a blind man and begged Jesus to touch him. He took the blind man by the hand and led him outside the village. When he had spit on the man's eyes and put his hands on him, Jesus asked, "Do you see anything?" He looked up and said, "I see people; they look like trees walking around." Once more Jesus put his hands on the man's eyes. Then his eyes were opened, his sight was restored, and he saw everything clearly. Jesus sent him home, saying, "Don't even go into the village."

What was it about this man or about his blindness that the Lord had to touch his eyes twice rather than only once? This is not the only blind person He healed. We have in John 9 the Lord's encounter with a man born blind, thus presenting a more difficult challenge in terms of gifting him with the ability to see! It cannot be that healing a blind person who one day was a seer would be more challenging than creating sight for someone who had never had it. And as noted above, if nature and even death itself could not stand in the face of His authority or power, what is it about this man from Bethsaida that Jesus had to touch his eyes two times rather than once in order for him to see clearly?

While there is no explicit discussion of faith in this story, one could argue that if anyone had faith, it would be those people and not the blind man himself. They were the ones to bring him to Jesus, similar to the four men who carried the paralytic and dropped him down from the roof before Jesus, according to Mark 2. Except in this case, the Lord did not commend their faith, as He did the other four men, despite the fact that these men not only brought the blind man to Jesus but also begged Him to touch him.

Some details in this story are worthy of our attention, beginning with the Galilean village, where this took place. That village was Bethsaida. The name of this town appears several times in Scripture. It was a village where the Lord Jesus initially performed a good number of miracles (see Matthew 11:21). Three of the twelve disciples—Philip, Andrew, and Peter, his brother—claimed this village their home (see John 1:44). Yet, according to the same verse in Matthew 11:21, the Lord pronounced a very hard judgment against this town, only second to Chorazin. "'Woe to you, Chorazin! Woe to you, Bethsaida! For if the miracles that were performed in you had been performed in Tyre and Sidon, they would have repented long ago in sackcloth and ashes.'"

Two more interconnected observations we make from the text are the fact that Jesus took the blind man and walked him outside the village; then, after healing him, He warned him not to go into it.

We do not know the exact reasons why Jesus did both. We can safely assume that for this miracle to take place, it was necessary for Jesus to lead the man outside Bethsaida. And even then, the miracle had to be performed by installments rather than all at once.

It seems there was such colossal unbelief and such strong rejection of Jesus—this is why He pronounced judgment in Matthew 11:21—that part of that judgment was for Jesus to discontinue performing miracles in the village. This could explain the reason he led the blind man outside Bethsaida. His message in that village was refused. They had chosen to reject Him. So, He did what He had told the disciples to do on their first mission, according to Matthew 10:14-15, wherein He said, "If anyone will not welcome you or listen to your words, leave that home or town and shake the dust off your feet. Truly I tell you, it will be more bearable for Sodom and Gomorrah on the day of judgment than for that town.'"

Moreover, by issuing a warning to the man not to go back into town, Jesus was disallowing any further testimony of Himself or of His power and authority therein. Jesus had performed a good number of miracles in that village before, as His words in Matthew 11:21 reveal. The inhabitants of that village had multiple testimonies from numerous individuals of all sorts of miracles taking place. They had chosen to flout these and scorn and treat them with contempt. Jesus was emphatic in his words to this man, telling him not to enter that town and not to render testimony. Here is how the literal Greek text would read that verse: "'Neither in the village you may be entering, nor you may be telling to anyone in the village.'" Sadly, there was nothing more in store for Bethsaida but judgment.

Before we look into what potential lessons the Lord sought to teach His disciples, we briefly look into the gradual healing the Lord granted this blind person. We may never understand the true reason why Christ touched this man twice, when He could have healed him with a word from His mouth. But it behooves us to give this further thought, as we look again at the text.

It is clear from the previous text that this blind man did not exercise any faith in Jesus. He was brought to Jesus, possibly with some hesitation on his part. We read of other blind men, such as Bartimaeus, who would not be silenced as he sought mercy from the Lord. Mark tells us in 10:48, and the verses, that follow that the more the crowd rebuked Bartimaeus and told him to be quiet, the more he shouted. And when Jesus called for him, he rose to his feet, threw his cloak away, and came to Him. Nothing was to stop him from asking to receive his sight.

This blind man of Bethsaida seems to be at the other end of the faith spectrum. He had no motivation to see again. He had given up on that. To him, there was no point trying, only to lose hope again. He had learned and had accepted life with that missing fifth sense. While there was nothing to stop Bartimaeus from coming to Jesus, there was nothing motivating this blind man from Bethsaida to seek Him. He had to be brought; otherwise, he would never have come on his own. Contrary to Bartimaeus, who seemingly was an outgoing, risk-taking individual, willing to sit out on public roads, this man from Bethsaida had resigned to his fate, probably waiting to die hopeless and helpless.

And so, the first time that Jesus laid his hands on his eyes, it was more to infuse hope to his soul than sight to his eyes. It was more to impassion him and arouse the dying sense of sight than to make him see. This is why Jesus seems to be performing this miracle by increments, using each one to stir up one aspect of this man's outlook. As the man opened his eyes for the first time after many years of blindness, he said he saw people like trees, walking around. Jesus had succeeded in rekindling the fire, or stirring the embers that had faded in this man's life. This man could not see for years and had given up on that completely. Now that his eyes have been opened, now that his hope has been reinvigorated, he is not satisfied until he sees clearly.

That first touch also purposed to arouse a sense of faith in this man. He was most probably influenced by the general outlook of his village toward Jesus. Granting him full recovery and a clear eyesight from the first touch, when he did not exercise any faith at all, may be counterproductive. Jesus was wetting his appetite, so to speak, by opening his eyes and letting him know that He can do something for him. By allowing him to see, even though it was cloudy, Jesus meant to plant the seed of faith in his heart and then give that seed a chance to germinate.

Since Jesus was preparing His disciples to carry the message after Him, that leaves no doubt, as we have seen in previous chapters, but to expect that through this encounter with the blind man, He also had things to teach them. This becomes very clear, as we consider the question that Jesus asked him: "'Do you see anything?'"

Why would Jesus ask this question? He had never asked anyone what effect His touch had on him or her. Unless, of course, Jesus was not asking just to hear the answer. He knew whether the man could see, and He knew what and how much he could see. What Jesus was doing by asking this question was inviting the witnesses, mainly the Twelve, to listen in. Now that He had their attention, He would continue chatting with this man and offer not one but several messages and lessons to His followers.

One potential message for the disciples was that there would come a time when God would cease sending messengers to the world, in the same way that Jesus denied the now healed man from going back into Bethsaida and giving testimony of what God did for him. Paul and Barnabas faced this situation as Luke records it in Acts 13:46, where both men confronted their Jewish audience, saying, "Since you reject it and do not consider yourselves worthy of eternal life, we now turn to the Gentiles."

Like this blind man, Peter was also from Bethsaida. Also like him, Peter needed a second touch, not to have his physical sight restored, but to be restored after he denied his Lord. It was after the Lord's resurrection that Peter decided to go back fishing at the same lake where Jesus had met and called him three plus years prior. Early the next morning, Jesus stood on the shore, waiting for Peter and his friends to come to shore with their empty nets. This was a rerun of an earlier experience, except that time, according to Luke 5, the Lord had gone into Peter's boat. This time, he simply stood on the shore and directed the men to where the fish was plentiful. Following a personal exchange with Peter, the Lord once again called Peter to follow Him (John 21:19). That was Peter's second touch! Second call! It becomes obvious that the second touch was not reflecting the Lord's inability to heal the blind man the first time he laid His hand on his eyes. Rather, it had to do with some obstinate habits that require not one but repetitive touches.

Again reflecting on the difference between Bartimaeus and this blind man from Bethsaida, the disciples could possibly glean that not every person they would later come in contact with would respond in the same way. Some, like Bartimaeus, would jump to the occasion and sprint, as they respond to the message of Christ. Others would have to be almost dragged to it.

Many among us will probably identify with this blind man from Bethsaida, having experienced the need for second touches and having discovered the need for renewed grace in our own lives. Hopefully, this will lead us, as we mature in the Lord to be more gracious toward others and to extend to them second chances in their Christian walk. It was in that same spirit that Paul wrote to the Galatian Christians (6:1-2), "Brothers and sisters, if someone is caught in a sin, you who live by the Spirit should restore that person gently. But watch yourselves, or you also may be tempted. Carry each other's burdens, and in this way you will fulfill the law of Christ."

CHAPTER X

THE GREAT COMMISSION
AND THE GREATER COMMISSION

THE GREAT COMMISSION

It has been customary for Bible students and commentators to consider the Great Commission as the ultimate climax in mission terminology and, therefore, to compare or contrast every other missionary expression with it. Yet, there is a great disservice to the Old Testament and to its Author were we to follow in the same pattern. For if God is consistent in His character, in His plan for His creation, and in His expectations regarding man's involvement in that plan, it would seem only normal that the Great Commission, like other fundamental expressions of faith and practice, be consistent with what preceded it in the Old Testament text.

Mission in the life of Israel as a nation was existential to a large degree. Their very life was to be a witness of their God, not in the sense of speaking that witness, but of living it. Their commission was to be a, "light to the nations."

The question that we will consider in this chapter is how much does the Great Commission, in particular, lend itself to such a perspective as stated previously in terms of its missionary emphasis.

In the last chapter of his gospel and the very last verses, 18-20, Matthew records for us what has been widely known as the Great Commission. At every other Christian conference on missions, these verses are quoted in an effort to mobilize the church at large to be involved in local and global missions. It is worth noting that the great missionary William Carey, also called the Father of Modern Missions, based his missionary zeal and career on this one text of Scripture.

In the English language text of the Great Commission that follows, we come across eight verb forms, which I have italicized.

> Then Jesus came to them and said, "All authority in heaven and on earth *has been given* to me. Therefore *go* and *make disciples* of all nations, *baptizing* them in the name of the Father and of the Son and of the Holy Spirit, and *teaching* them *to obey* everything I have *commanded* you. And surely *I am* with you always, to the very end of the age."

The translation quoted above, as well as a number of other English and non-English translations, render the verb "go" in the imperative tense. That, in turn, has translated into a strong emphasis on the "going" element of the commission. Thus, there can be no commission without journeying or traveling, irrespective of the distance traveled, be it measured in a few feet or in thousands of miles. The importance of the going element is underscored by the reference to "all nations,", *ta ethne*, since Christians cannot possibly impact all nations if they did not go to them. That general sense is further compounded on reading the Lord's final words before He was taken up to heaven, according to chapter 1 of the book of Acts. There, He promised His disciples power from above once the Holy Spirit came on them, and added, "'and you will be my witnesses in Jerusalem, and in all Judea and Samaria, and to the ends of the earth'" (Acts 1:8).

This promise carries within it a well-defined and identifiable geographical progression. Added to the commission in Matthew 28, and the whole notion of Christ's mission to His church is certain to carry as much weight for such geographical progression as other elements of the mission, and possibly even more. Paul's missionary *journeying,* as recorded in Acts, can only accentuate and confirm such an understanding of the church's mission.

Yet, for all the emphasis placed on that verb, it is quite striking to note that such rhetoric is undermined by the fact that the verb "go" is not in the imperative tense, as has been widely understood. The Greek form of the verb, transliterated into English as *poreuthentes,* is literally best translated "being gone." The going sense in that commission is an activity to be taken for granted, a general assumption that reflects one's natural moves in performing the miscellaneous activities of one's life. The "going" is not and has never been the focus of the mandate as it was given by our Lord. This is not meant in any way to disqualify those who are "sent" or those who go to nearby fields of ministry or to fields beyond the seas. This is meant to point out that we are all *on the go,* purposefully making disciples, regardless of where we may be—in our homes or in foreign fields of Christian ministry.

The disturbing distortion that the mishandling of the Great Commission has sadly bred is that at a time when every Christian is called to be actively engaged in mission, regardless of his or her profession, a separate classification of Christians has resulted for whom the word "missionary" was coined, with the understanding that being a missionary meant one thing and one thing only: "being sent." The end result became a compartmentalization of Christians into missionaries and nonmissionaries: the sent ones and those who have not been called to go. And beyond that, the compartmentalization of the Christian life into a time when one is engaged as a goer in such a class of service and when one is not. It is worth noting that the term "missionary" did not appear in Scripture. It is also worth noting that Paul, in the diverse lists of spiritual gifts that he presented in his letters to the Romans, the Corinthians, and to the Ephesians, did not include such a gift. This is not to mean that the exercise of mission is not biblical. Rather, it means that it is incumbent on every Christian, and not designated or specified to one class of individuals called missionaries, for while each of us may have a different profession, our calling is one and the same. It cannot be that the missionary God of the Old Testament, Who has called *all* Israel to be a light to the nations, would only invite a certain class of the church to be engaged with Him in the same fashion in the New Testament. The invitation is to everyone.

A more dangerous result of the historical emphasis on the going part of the commission, by making that an imperative, is the partial if not complete oversight of the one and only imperative in that commission, namely, the "making of disciples." This theme is thus the unique, exclusive, and central part of the Great Commission. If anything, the Lord was commissioning his disciples to do exactly what he did during his earthly ministry, which was inviting them to follow him and turning them from simple followers to committed disciples, from Christians to priests, from learners to teachers, and from followers to imitators of Himself. This is the heart and soul of what the Lord commissioned his disciples to do.

It is worth noting in this context that the Lord did not explain his marching orders to His disciples. He did not have to unpack for them what He meant by the imperative to make disciples. They had lived through that process and knew firsthand His intent.

The only logical conclusion is that defining the commission or the Christian's mission as simply the act of sending or the act of going is too narrow.

As we further explore this commission, we come across a number of other important, and to some people, foreign truths. First, we discover that the disciple-making process, as with the Lord and the twelve, begins right at the start of the relationship between a master or a teacher and a potential follower or learner. The twelve were Jews in every sense of the word, as was explained in previous chapters. While it is true that they forsook everything to follow Jesus, that did not automatically make them believers. We cannot tell, and the Gospel writers do not explicitly elaborate or enter into any detail of when each placed his faith in Christ. Each of them most probably had his own personal moment when he discovered the truth about his Master.

I wonder if, in the case of Peter, the moment of truth was when he fell on his knees in his boat and asked the Lord to go away from him, admitting that he was a sinful person (see Luke 5:8). That would place his conversion experience early in Jesus' ministry! If that were the case, we will need to leave room in the years that follow for moments of doubt, hesitation, and denial. It could also be argued that Peter's conversion experience was not one that could be pinned down to a specific moment or time; that it was progressive.

Or as we think of Thomas, it is plausible to imagine his faith finally rooted when he goes on his knees before the Risen Lord and exclaims, "My Lord and my God!" (John 20:28). If so, that would place his faith toward the very end of Jesus' ministry. Others of the Twelve were initially followers of John the Baptist, and it was only over time that their allegiance changed, and their faith in Jesus as Messiah was deepened.

The point here, nonetheless, is that it can hardly be argued that any of the twelve believed in Jesus as Messiah, Savior, or Lord before following Him, which means that the disciple-making process is one that will first and foremost engage non-believers, in the same way that the Lord Jesus invited the twelve and others to engage with Him. Understood in that way, verbal evangelism becomes only a small part of that process. Our study in the previous chapters underlined the multifaceted aspects of what true incarnational disciple-making is all about.

To substantiate the claim that disciple-making engages non-believers first and foremost, we turn once again to the Great Commission and pay special notice to the sequence of activities Jesus commissioned his disciples to perform. Go back to Matthew 20:19, where Jesus said, "'Therefore go and make disciples of all nations, baptizing them in the name of the Father and of the Son and of the Holy Spirit.'" Immediately following the imperative to make disciples comes baptism.

If disciple-making were what many make it to be today, which is courses on how to pray or how to study God's Word or other aspects of Christian growth, baptism would have to precede that process rather than come after it. But since disciple-making is engaging non-believers, leading them to the Lord mostly by way of actualizing the message before them, it only makes sense that baptism would directly follow. This confirms again the basic notion that disciple-making targets non-believers in the first place.

It is only after people are drawn or discipled into the Christian faith, and after they receive baptism, that the teaching process begins. Baptized disciples would have already seen in their disciplers how they live by faith, how they walk in the Spirit, how they study the Word, how they pray, and many other aspects of a mature Christian life. The role of the discipler at that point is to teach and lead by example and by word, so the disciples can become imitators of him or her and begin to engage non-believers in the same process of disciple-making.

Sadly, for one reason or another, many churches, agencies, and individual Christians have freely interchanged the two terms "disciple-making" and "teaching" as if both were one and the same. Such muddling is at best confusing! Why would the Lord repeat Himself in the same sentence? Such muddling is also very misleading. By attributing to the process of disciple-making the notion of Christian growth and maturing as happens through teaching, we would completely disregard what disciple-making is all about, and thus save ourselves the cost involved in that worthy process.

Disciple-making is the calling of Christ on every life and on all of life. We cannot continue to separate our personal or collective spirituality from other dimensions of our lives by means of compartmentalization. Disciple-making, as presented in the Great Commission, involves *all* of life in *all* of its ages, stages, and circumstances and not one small segment of it. It is either all or none.

Back in the early nineties, I received an unsolicited letter from my then one hundred-year-old dad. That was not the first letter he wrote to me, but it was a unique letter. Now that he has gone to be with the Lord, I treasure it and continue to refer back to it for lessons from life. My dad did not receive much formal education. His dad, my grandfather, was more interested to see his only son make money and establish a home to bring him grandsons than seeing his son receive an education. But my dad was cultured. At a time when means of transportation in Palestine, and the Middle East in general, were very rudimentary and limited, he had traveled to Syria, Lebanon, and Jordan, among other countries. His love for travel did not depart from him even in his old age, having made an intercontinental trip from his home in Jerusalem to the United States at one hundred years of age.

In that one letter, my dad once again complained about the lack of education he had received. He complained about the rough life he had with his first wife, my mother, and the mistreatment he received from his in-laws. He also complained at the absence of communication from his sons, my brothers. The one positive note in the letter was the fact that inviting Jesus into his life in his mid-seventies had brought rays of hope and a trust in what God must have planned for him. At the time, my dad had no inkling that he would live to be one of the oldest people, if not the oldest, living on earth. He went into the Lord's presence twenty-six days after celebrating his 119th birthday. What a full life he had lived.

What was most amazing in this letter was the fact that for my dad, life was not compartmentalized to the degree that there were no paragraphs, no full stops, and no commas in the letter. Nothing! It was all one, very long sentence. It was his life story as he recalled it, played out before me on one handwritten page. His birth to old Palestinian peasants; his work at the Samaritan Monastery, next to Jacob's Well in Samaria; his draft in the First World War; his marriage to my mother; the sons and daughters born to him; the death of his wife; and every other detail that the page could possibly contain. It was all breathed out in one long sentence. I had not known my dad as a good storyteller until that day, when sitting behind my desk in Southern Europe, I teared up reading his confessions! My formal education was not lacking. I had amassed years of college and university education on a number of campuses in a number of countries. But I had not seen life the same way my dad had seen it. To me, life was categorized and compartmentalized. But not to him. Life was undivided. Life is undivided.

Though the Lord did not leave us with a handwritten manuscript, undivided by commas or full stops, or broken into paragraphs, we know from Scripture that He also lived with a single objective, around which he built all of his life. Once that objective was fulfilled, there did not seem to be any reason for Him to live. This is why, in commissioning His disciples, there was a singularity of purpose. All they were to do was to aim at one thing and one thing only: making disciples. And if and since the Lord had chosen to use that single method in his three short years of ministry, how much more should we make that our priority and calling.

THE GREATER COMMISSION

Reading the above title could raise a few eyebrows. What *Greater Commission* could there be than what we have in Matthew 28:18-20? To answer that question, I invite you to look with me at the prayer of the Lord Jesus in the gospel of John, chapter 17.

After Jesus said this, he looked toward heaven and prayed: "Father, the time has come. Glorify your Son, that your Son may glorify you. For you granted him authority over all people that he might give eternal life to all those you have given him. Now this is eternal life: that they may know you, the only true God, and Jesus Christ, whom you have sent. *I have brought you glory on earth by completing the work you gave me to do. And now, Father, glorify me in your presence with the glory I had with you before the world began mine.*

"I have revealed you to those whom you gave me out of the world. They were yours; you gave them to me and they have obeyed your word. Now they know that everything you have given me comes from you. For I gave them the words you gave me and they accepted them. They knew with certainty that I came from you, and they believed that you sent me. I pray for them. I am not praying for the world, but for those you have given me, for they are yours. All I have is yours, and all you have is mine. And glory has come to me through them. I will remain in the world no longer, but they are still in the world, and I am coming to you. Holy Father, protect them by the power of your name—the name you gave me—so that they may be one as we are one. While I was with them, I protected them and kept them safe by that name you gave me. None has been lost except the one doomed to destruction so that Scripture would be fulfilled.

"I am coming to you now, but I say these things while I am still in the world, so that they may have the full measure of my joy within them. I have given them your word and the world has hated them, for they are not of the world any more than I am of the world. My prayer is not that you take them out of the world but that you protect them from the evil one. They are not of the world, even as I am not of it. Sanctify them by the truth; your word is truth. As you sent me into the world, I have sent them into the world. For them I sanctify myself, that they too may be truly sanctified."

This chapter has a total of twenty-six verses. Of those, Jesus dedicated the first nineteen verses, quoted above, to pray for the twelve. The references to them are vivid and clear and bear no ambiguity. Yet, there is one specific verse that requires special attention and study, namely verse 4, italicized above.

Jesus had not died yet. He had not completed the mission for which He came: offering Himself as a sacrifice. So, what was He referring to when He stated, according to that verse, "'I have brought you glory on earth by *completing the work* you gave me to do'"? The King James Version renders the verse as follows: "'I have glorified thee on the earth: I have *finished the work* which Thou gavest me to do" (italics mine).

The Greek verb for "finished" or "completed" is *tetelestai*, which is the same word that the Lord used while hanging on the cross, according to John 19:30. At that instant, the work of redemption was being completed, and soon after, He surrendered His Spirit to the Father.

That cannot be said of His prayer in John 17:4. That finished or completed work cannot refer to the act of redemption. The cross was still in front of Him. So, what work was the Lord referring to? What work had He already completed?

The immediate context leaves no doubt but to believe that He was referring to preparing His disciples. His prayer, almost exclusively lifted up on behalf of His disciples, details some aspects of that finished work: He revealed the Father to them (verse 6). He gave them the words that the Father gave Him (verse 8). He gave them His word (verse 14). He sent them into the world (verse 18). He has sanctified Himself that they may be truly sanctified (verse 19).

These different aspects are all encompassed in the term "disciple-making." Jesus had called them, taught them, lived with them, and before them, sanctified and sent them. He had finished His work in them. That process was completed in three years. The one remaining element would be the outpouring of the Holy Spirit, which Jesus would send once He was lifted up.

We note also that Jesus refers to that as "_the_ work" that the Father gave him. In other words, the commission that the Father had given the Son was to come to earth and make disciples. And once that work was finished, there was nothing else for Jesus to do but to die on a cross. His earthly ministry was basically over!

We spend ten, twenty, or many more years in ministry, and until the Holy Spirit of God shines in our hearts and brings these truths home, we go on thinking that our role is to just do more evangelism, more preaching, or teaching. We completely forgo and forget that the Great Commission of making disciples is but an exact copy of the Father's _Greater Commission_ to His Son. What ministry could have more priority over that? If that were the Son's commission, it definitely makes much sense to be ours, too.

It follows that the Great Commission is but a reflection of the greater commission of the Father. This is what the Lord Jesus had said in no unclear terms: "'As the Father has sent me, I am sending you'" (John 20:21). And so, as our Lord dedicated his three short years of earthly ministry to pouring His life into the Twelve, so are we called to pour our lives. That is the heart and soul of what making disciples is about. This is incarnational disciple-making the Jesus way!

Giacomo Puccini was the most famous Italian opera composer after Verdi. He was born in 1858. He wrote sixteen operas, most of which are performed to this day. The one that caught my attention was *Turandot,* which he began working on in early 1920. By March of 1924, he had completed the opera up to the final touches. In October of 1924, he was diagnosed with cancer, for which he went to Brussels, Belgium, for treatment. On November 24, Puccini underwent surgery, and a few days later, he died of complications.

Puccini left behind tens of pages of sketches for the end of *Turandot.* A certain Alfano interpreted those sketches. One year and five months after Puccini's death, the musical opera was conducted by the famous Arturo Toscanini. In the middle of Act III, the orchestra rested. It is said that Toscanini stopped and laid down his baton. He turned to the audience and announced in Italian, *"Qui termina la rappresentazione. Perché a questo punto, il maestro è morto"* (Here the performance ends. Because at this point, the maestro died).

The curtain was lowered slowly. Then, Toscanini picked up his baton and exclaimed, "But his disciples finished his work." The disciples had picked up where the maestro had stopped.

The Great Commission is only a reflection of the Greater Commission, and that, if anything, should be your mission and mine! Our commission is picking up, as it were, where our Maestro had stopped! That mission was not only dying for a dying world, but making disciples of the living.